PA-28 Warrior
A Pilot's Guide

Jeremy M. Pratt

Aviation Supplies & Academics, Inc.
Newcastle, Washington

U.S. Edition 1995

© 1995 Aviation Supplies & Academics, Inc.

First published in England by Airplan Flight Equipment, Ltd.
and Jeremy M. Pratt, 1992

PA-28 Warrior: A Pilot's Guide
Jeremy M. Pratt

ASA-PG-PA-28W
ISBN 1-56027-214-7

Aviation Supplies & Academics, Inc.
Newcastle, Washington

Printed in the United States of America

02 01   9 8 7 6 5 4 3

Library of Congress Cataloging-in-Publication Data:

Pratt, Jeremy M.
    PA-28 Warrior / Jeremy M. Pratt. — U.S. ed.
        p.   cm.   — (A pilot's guide)
    Includes index.
    ISBN 1-56027-214-7
    1. Piper PA-28 (Private planes) I. Title. II. Series: Pratt, Jeremy M. Pilot's guide.
    TL686.P5P732 1995
    629.132'5217—dc20   95-13961
                                                      CIP

Acknowledgements

I would like to thank all those whose knowledge, help and advice went into this book; in particular:

Airspeed Aviation
Air Nova
Simon Booth
CAA Safety Promotion Section
CSE Aviation
Colourmatch
Adrian Dickinson
Steve Dickinson
David Hockings
Andy Holland
Phil Huntington

Wendy Mellor
Manchester School of Flying
Margaret Parkes
Paul Price
Ravenair
Neil Rigby
John Ross
Ian Sixsmith
John Thorpe
Visual Eyes

Sarah, Kate and Miles

Jeremy M. Pratt
August 1992

Contents

Section 3 – Handling the Piper PA-28 Warrior

Section 4 – Mixture and Carburetor Icing Supplement

Section 5 – Expanded PA-28 Pre-Flight Checklist

Section 6 – Loading and Performance

Section 7 – Conversions

Index

Editor's Note

Welcome to ASA's *A Pilot's Guide* series by Jeremy Pratt. In this guide, you'll learn from the experts the general principles involved in flying the PA-28 Warrior, with extra insight on individual characteristics gleaned from flying experience.

PA-28 Warrior: A Pilot's Guide is not an authoritative document. Material in this book is presented for the purposes of orientation, familiarization, and comparison only.

Performance figures are based upon the indicated weights, standard atmospheric conditions, level hard-surface dry runways, and no wind. They are values based upon calculations derived from flight tests conducted by the aircraft company under carefully documented conditions and using professional test pilots. Performance will vary with individual aircraft and numerous other factors affecting flight.

The approved *Pilot's Operating Handbook* and/or the approved *Airplane Flight Manual* is the only source of authoritative information for any individual aircraft. In the interests of safety and good airmanship, the pilot should be familiar with these documents.

Section 1
General Description

PA-28 Warrior A Pilot's Guide

Introduction to the PA-28 Warrior

WARRIOR—a North American Indian experienced in battle

The Warrior, described by Piper as the logical progression from the PA-28 Cherokee series, was first introduced in 1974. The most obvious difference is the re-designed, semi-tapered wing, which contrasts strongly against the constant chord wing of the earlier models (known variously as the "Hershey bar" wing or plank wing for obvious reasons). This new wing gave handling, speed and payload advantages and, in addition, the cabin was bigger. In later years "Velour" style interiors also became available as an option.

The semi-tapered wing of the Warrior is markedly different from the Cherokee constant chord wing.

The Warrior I, in production from 1974 to 1977, is powered by a Lycoming 0-320 engine of 150 HP. The Warrior II, introduced in 1977, has an increased Maximum Takeoff Weight (MTOW) and a 160 HP version of the 0-320 engine. The Cadet, essentially a stripped-down trainer version of the Warrior II, was introduced in 1987.

The Archer II, first built in 1976, features a 180 HP engine, and a better payload capability than the Warrior, making it a good touring proposition. Both the Warrior and Archer were introduced to compete in a market dominated by the Cessna 172. They both offer certain advantages in the cabin comfort, but ultimately the buying decision often comes down to a simple preference for high or low wing aircraft. Since the Cessna 172 ceased production, Piper has had, in theory, a virtual monopoly in the market for four-seater touring aircraft. In fact many Warriors have become part of flight school fleets, which is the reason for the Cadet development. This book deals primarily with the Warrior II, with reference to the Cadet and Archer II, where differences occur. Much of the information is also relevant to the Warrior I.

MODEL YEAR	MODEL	PRODUCTION NAME
1974 – 1977	PA-28-151	Warrior

MODEL YEAR	MODEL	PRODUCTION NAME
1977 – 1994	PA-28-161	Warrior II

MODEL YEAR	MODEL	PRODUCTION NAME
1976 – 1994	PA-28-181	Archer II

MODEL YEAR	MODEL	PRODUCTION NAME
1987 – 1993	PA-28-161	Cadet

The Airframe

The PA-28 airframe is generally described as being of all metal construction. The primary structure is constructed of aluminum alloy, with the engine mount made from tubular steel. Some non-structural components such as the wing tips and landing gear fairings are made from fiberglass.

The fuselage has a semi-monocoque structure; that is, the vertical bulkheads and frames are joined by horizontal longerons and stringers which run the length of the fuselage. The metal skin is riveted to the longerons and stringers; this arrangement is conventional for modern light aircraft and allows loads to be spread over the whole construction. At the rear of the fuselage the tail unit incorporates an "all moving" tailplane, or stabilator. Underneath the rear fuselage, a triangular combined tie-down point and tail guard is fitted.

The wings are of cantilever design (unsupported by external struts or bracing) and have a positive dihedral. The wing is semi-tapered with a laminar flow airfoil section. The wing main spars butt to a spar carry-through box which is an integral part of the fuselage structure. This structure runs under the rear seats and in effect provides a continuous main spar. On the upper surface of the right wing a black walkway is marked; this is the only area of the wing to be walked on or stood on. Underneath each wing a metal ring is fitted to be used as a tie-down point.

The tail tie-down point.

The wing main spar at the wing root.

The spar carry-through box, seen here on a disassembled Warrior.

The Flight Controls

Dual flight controls are installed as standard and link the cockpit controls to the control surface via cable linkages.

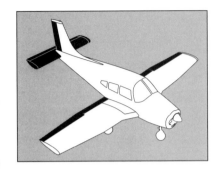

The AILERONS are of the differential type, moving upward through 25° and downward through 12.5° (from 1976 models on). A balance weight is fitted on a short rod at the outer end of each aileron, and this weight is visible inside the wing tip cavity.

The FLAPS are of the simple slotted type. They are manually operated from a lever between the cockpit seats, and through a torque tube and push rods to the flap surfaces. Four positions can be selected, fully up (0°), 10°, 25° and 40°. The flaps lock in the full up position, and only in this position can the walkway on the right hand flap be stood upon. In any other position the flaps will move rapidly down to 40° if any weight is placed on the right flap walkway, dumping the unwary onto the ground! The button on the end of the flap lever is depressed to retract the flaps.

The RUDDER is operated from the rudder pedals (which are also linked to the steerable nose wheel) and can move through 27° either side of the neutral position. A rudder trim wheel is fitted in the cockpit below the instrument panel. This wheel is spring-loaded to trim out excessive rudder forces in flight. The rudder trim control turns clockwise to give nose-right trim and counter-clockwise to give nose-left trim. As the rudder is connected (via rods from the rudder pedals) to the nose wheel, the control surface cannot be moved while the aircraft is stationary without exerting considerable force—this is not recommended.

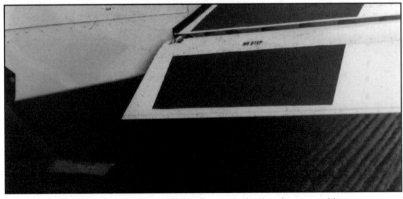

Do not step on the flap walkway if the flaps are in the down position.

The Warrior has an all moving STABILATOR, which functions as a combined stabilizer and elevator; it moves up 14° from neutral and down 2° from neutral. The control functions in the natural sense, and by design provides a very powerful pitching force. As part of its design the stabilator incorporates an ANTI-BALANCE TAB at its trailing edge, sometimes referred to as an anti-servo tab. This tab combines two functions. It moves in the same direction as the stabilator to provide a "damping" force, increasing the feel of the control, which is very important with such a powerful control surface. In addition, the anti-balance tab acts as a trim tab to trim out pitch forces on the control wheel; the control surface moves 3° up from neutral and 12° down from neutral. The cockpit control for the trim tab is a conventional trim wheel located on the cockpit floor between the seats, and acts in the normal sense, rotating the wheel forward to trim nose down and backward to trim nose up. Many Warriors and Archers are also equiped with an electric trim button on the control wheel.

The all-moving stabilator and anti-balance tab.

The Landing Gear

The Warrior LANDING GEAR is fixed and is a tricycle-type; the main landing gear has a track of 10 feet.

The main landing gear incorporates an air-oil oleo strut to absorb operating loads. Normally, the main gear struts should have about 4.5 inches of the piston tube exposed under normal static load (aircraft with full fuel and oil). The Warrior I and first year (1977) Warrior IIs have standard wheel fairings on the main and nose wheels. From 1978 models on, the main and nose landing gear have a full fairing, which joins the wheel fairings. The Cadet has no wheel or landing gear fairings. The main landing gear is fitted with 6.00 X 6 wheels.

The nose gear attaches to the engine mount and also has an air/oil oleo strut to damp and absorb the normal operating loads. Normally, about 3.25 inches of the piston tube should be exposed. On the rear of the nose strut a torque link is installed to maintain the correct alignment of the nose wheel, its lower arm is fitted to the nose wheel fork and the upper arm to the oleo cylinder casing. The nose gear is steerable through direct linkage to the rudder pedals. A spring device aids nose wheel and rudder center- ing and is also adjustable to act as the rudder trim (see "Rudder," page 1-7). Bungee springs are incorporated in the nose wheel steering mecha- nism to aid lighter and smoother nose wheel steering.

The nose wheel has a range of movement 30° either side of straight ahead (20° on the Cadet). The nose wheel tire is a 5.00 X 5 unit on the Warrior, and a 6.00 X 6 unit on the Archer II. In common with just about all light aircraft, the nose gear is not as strong as the main gear. The tire

A fully-faired main landing gear.

A faired nose wheel assembly.

grooves should have at least 1/16 inch depth over 75% of the tire to be serviceable. Additionally, if the tread across the width of the tire is worn to less than 1/16 inch in any one place, the tire will need replacing.

The BRAKE system consists of single disc brake assemblies fitted to each main wheel and operated by a hydraulic system. The brake lever located below the center of the instrument panel operates a master cylinder located below and behind the control panel. When the control is pulled back braking is evenly applied to both main wheels. A small button on the side of the brake lever allows it to be locked in the ON position to act as a parking brake. To release the parking brake the control is pulled back (which unlatches the button), and then pushed full forward. When toe brakes are fitted, they are operated by depressing the upper half of the rudder pedal. In this system each toe brake has a separate brake cylinder above the pedal, and it is possible to operate the brakes differentially—to the left or right wheel. This system allows the aircraft to turn in a very tight circle, and it is possible to lock one main wheel with the use of some pedal force. Turning around a wheel in this fashion tends to "scrub" the tire and is generally discouraged. A

The brake fluid reservoir on the upper left firewall.

brake fluid reservoir which feeds to all the brake cylinders is fitted to the upper left forward face of the firewall (accessed via the left engine cowling). Here it can be inspected for fluid level and replenished if necessary.

The Engine

The Warrior I (1974 – 1977) is fitted with a Lycoming 0-320-E engine of 150 HP at 2,700 RPM. The Warrior II (including CADET) has a Lycoming 0-320-D engine giving 160 HP at 2,700 RPM. The Archer II has a Lycoming 0-360-A engine of 180 HP at 2,700 RPM. The 320 and 360 designators refer to the cubic capacity of the engine in inches. Apart from this

difference, the engine models are similar and are treated as one subject below.

The engine is a four cylinder unit, with cylinders horizontally opposed across the crankshaft. The cylinders are staggered so that each connecting rod has its own crankshaft throw. They are steel barrels with aluminum alloy cylinder heads screwed on with interference fits.

The engine is air-cooled. Airflow enters the engine compartment at the front of the cowling, and is directed by baffles to flow over the whole engine. The cylinders feature deep cooling fins to aid cooling; the airflow leaves the engine compartment at the rear lower cowling underneath the engine compartment.

The engine is mounted on a steel tubular mounting which attaches to the firewall.

When latching the cowling, note the top of the latch is under the tab on the cowling.

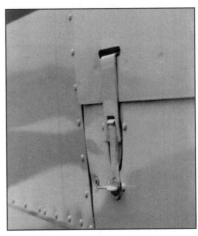

Cowling latch properly closed and locked with a half turn of the catch.

The Propeller

The propeller is an all metal, two bladed, fixed pitch design, turned by direct drive from the engine crankshaft; it rotates clockwise as seen from the cockpit. For the Warrior II and Cadet the diameter is 74", and the Archer II propeller has a diameter of 76".

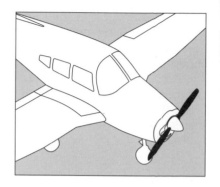

The Warrior propeller.

The Ignition System

The engine features a dual ignition system, fitted with two magnetos. The magnetos are small AC generators driven by the crankshaft rotation to provide a very high voltage to a distributor, which directs it via high voltage leads (or high tension leads) to the spark plugs. At the spark plug, the current must cross a gap; in doing so a spark is produced which ignites the fuel/air mixture in the cylinder.

The magnetos are fitted at the rear of the engine, one each side of the engine center line (hence, Left and Right magnetos). The usual arrangement is for each magneto to fire the bottom spark plugs of the two cylinders on one side of the engine and the top spark plugs on the other side. Each cylinder has two spark plugs (top and bottom) for safety and efficiency. The leads that run from the magnetos to the spark plugs should be secure and there should be no splits or cracks in the plastic insulation covering the leads.

It is worth emphasizing that the ignition system is totally independent of the aircraft electrical system, and once the engine is running it operates regardless of the serviceability of the battery or alternator.

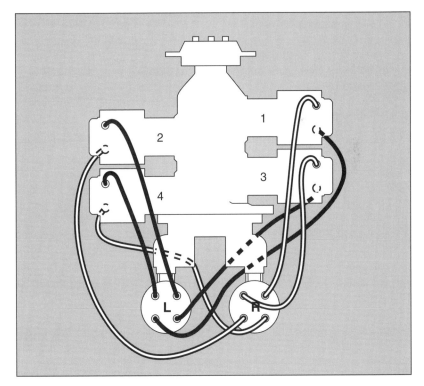

The Oil System

The engine's oil system provides lubrication, cooling, sealing, cleansing and protection against corrosion. The system is a wet-sump, pressure feed system with the oil sump located under the engine. Oil is drawn from here by the engine-driven oil pump, through a cooler and filter and into the oil gallery of the right half of the crankcase. When the oil has flowed around the engine it drains down to the sump by gravity. An oil pressure relief valve is fitted in the upper right side of the crankcase. The function of this valve is to maintain the correct operating pressure over a wide range of temperatures and RPM settings. Above a certain pressure, the valve will open and allow oil to return to the sump rather than continuing into the lubricating system.

Oil quantity can be checked on a dipstick which is accessible from the right hand side of the engine. The dipstick is graduated in U.S. quarts and measures the quantity of the oil sump. When the engine has been running, the oil will take up to 10 minutes to return to the

Oil filler tube.

sump, and only then can a true reading be taken. When replacing the dipstick care must be taken not to over-tighten the cap. To do so may make it exceptionally difficult to open the cap again, and it is possible to strip the thread on the cap or filler tube.

The oil temperature gauge and oil pressure gauge in the cockpit enable the pilot to monitor the health of the oil system.

The warning annuciator panel.

The Warriors and Archers (with the exception of the 1974 Warrior I models) are fitted with an annunciator panel at the top center of the instrument panel below the compass. This panel has three warning lights for VAC (vacuum), OIL (oil pressure) and ALT (electrical system). A test button is fitted to check the operation of the lights when the engine is running. The OIL warning light illuminates if oil pressure falls below 35 psi.

The Starter System

The starter motor is housed at the lower front left side of the engine. It incorporates a geared cog that engages with the teeth of the starter ring when the starter is operated. As the engine is turned, an impulse coupling in the left magneto operates, this retards the spark and aids starting. When the engine fires and begins to rotate under its own power this impulse coupling ceases to operate and normal spark timing is resumed. When the key is released, allowing the key to return to the BOTH position, the cog on the starter motor withdraws at a predetermined engine RPM to be clear of the starter ring.

The Fuel System

The Warrior has two aluminum fuel tanks, located in the inboard leading edge of each wing. From these tanks, a fuel line runs through the wing and fuselage to the fuel selector valve located on the left lower cockpit wall in the pilot footwell. From this valve, the fuel line runs through the firewall to a fuel strainer bowl mounted on the forward left face of the firewall. From the strainer bowl, a fuel line runs through the electric fuel pump and engine driven fuel pump to the carburetor. A separate line runs from the strainer bowl to the cockpit primer, and from there to three cylinders.

Two TANK VENTS, one for each fuel tank, protrude from the lower surface of each wing. The forward facing pipe vent ensures that ambient pressure is maintained above the fuel in the fuel tank. Should this vent become blocked, a vacuum may form in the tank as the fuel level lowers, and fuel flow to the engine may be interrupted.

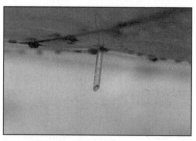

An underwing tank vent.

There are three FUEL STRAINERS (or quick drains), one at the lower rear inboard edge of each tank, accessible from the inboard lower wing surface, and one from the fuel bowl, accessed at the lower left cowling. Fuel can only be drawn from the bowl if the cockpit fuel selector is in the Left or Right position.

An underwing fuel strainer.

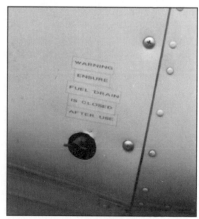

The engine fuel strainer with warning sign.

The shape of the fuel strainers has been the cause of problems. To take a fuel sample, the bar of the strainer is pushed up against a spring, and fuel will flow into the fuel tester. When the bar is released it should return to its original position, and the fuel flow ceases.

The original strainer has a "lip" which makes it possible for the valve to lock in the open position, and fuel to continue to drain through the valve even after the bar has been released. If this occurs to the tank strainers, the result will be the loss of fuel from the tanks, and possible fuel exhaustion.

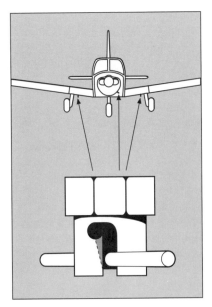

If the engine fuel strainer is open, the likely result is engine failure just after takeoff due to fuel starvation. In documented incidents where the fuel was *not* turned on for the fuel drain check, the fact that the engine fuel strainer was locked open was missed. The start, taxi, power checks and takeoff were normal, however the engine failed just after takeoff.

A recommended modification is for operators to file off an area of the strainer valve so that the bar cannot lock in the open position. Obviously, whether or not this modification has been carried out, care should be exercised when operating the fuel drains.

The cockpit fuel selector (selected "OFF").

The cockpit FUEL SELECTOR can also be a problem. The selector is located on the lower left cockpit wall of the pilot's footwell, and so is not easily accessible to a pilot in the right seat (an instructor, for example). Take care when moving the selector lever, since it is somewhat out of sight of the pilot. The selector can be used to feed the engine from either the Left or Right tank. To turn the fuel off, a spring loaded latch on the selector must first be depressed and then the lever rotated to the OFF position. This operation can be a two handed operation, which does help prevent the accidental selection of the OFF position.

In normal operation the fuel is drawn through the system by an engine driven FUEL PUMP. However, should this pump fail, the fuel supply to the carburetor will cease and the engine will stop. Therefore a second, electrical fuel pump is installed, and this pump is selected ON or OFF from a cockpit switch. Normally the electric fuel pump is selected ON during takeoff, landing, and when changing tanks. A fuel pressure gauge is fitted, reading from a sender between the engine driven fuel pump and the carburetor.

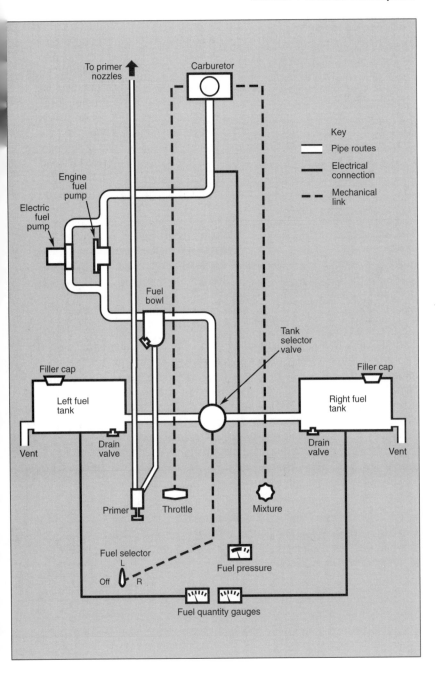

The Carburetor

The CARBURETOR mixes air with the fuel from the fuel system and supplies the fuel/air mix to the cylinders. The carburetor is located under the engine, and takes induction air from a scoop intake in the lower front cowling. This air is filtered and then fed into the carburetor air box. In this box, a butterfly valve is used to allow either the filtered or heated air to be fed to the carburetor. Heated air comes from an unfiltered inlet inside the front cowling which then passes into a shroud around the exhaust which heats it before it reaches the carburetor. Hot or cold air is selected via the carburetor heat control in the cockpit. The use of this control and the subject of carburetor icing are fully discussed in Section 4. From the carburetor, the fuel/air mix is carried to the induction manifold and to the inlet port of each cylinder.

The carburetor is fitted with an ACCELERATOR PUMP. With a normal carburetor, sudden opening of the throttle can cause the engine to falter due to an excessively lean mixture, or "lean mixture out." The accelerator pump introduces a charge of fuel when the throttle is suddenly opened to cure this problem. However, if the throttle is opened too quickly (for example, in under 2 seconds) the extra fuel can cause a "rich mixture out."

The PRIMER CONTROL, situated next to the throttle quadrant, is an aid to starting. The control is unlocked by rotating it until a pin on the shaft aligns with the cut-out in the collar. The control can then be pulled out, filling the primer with fuel from the fuel bowl. The primer is then pushed in, delivering fuel to the cylinder intake ports. For a cold engine, three cycles of the primer is usually sufficient. When priming is completed, the primer should be pushed fully in with the pin aligned with the collar cut-out, and then rotated about half a turn to lock. As a check, attempt to pull the primer out; it should remain locked. It is important that the primer is fully locked, otherwise engine rough running may result.

The MIXTURE is controlled from the mixture lever located in the cockpit which adjusts the fuel/air ratio in the carburetor. In the full forward position this control gives a RICH mixture, and if moved to the rearward ICO (Idle Cut-Off) position the fuel supply is cut off and the engine stops. The use of this control is covered in Section 4.

The power quadrant has a lever on its right side. Movement of this "friction" control adjusts the friction of the throttle and mixture levers, and allows for them to be kept in the desired position. Generally this lever is adjusted to leave the throttle and mixture with relatively loose and easy movement on the ground, but is tightened to hold the levers in position for takeoff.

The Electrical System

The Warrior has a 14 volt, direct
current (DC) electrical system. The
alternator is mounted to the front
lower right of the engine, and is
engine-driven from a belt drive off
a pulley directly behind the starter
ring. The alternator is rated at 60
amps; a 12 volt battery is located
inside a thermo-plastic box under
the rear seat on the right hand
side, or on the right forward face of

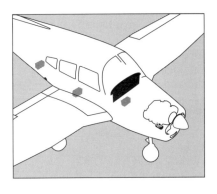

the firewall from 1983 models on. On the Archer aircraft, the battery is
located aft of the baggage compartment.

The ALTERNATOR is the primary source of power to the electrical system
in normal operations with the engine running. The alternator produces
alternating current (AC) which is converted into direct current by diodes
incorporated in the alternator housing which act as rectifiers. By their
design, alternators require a small voltage (about 3 volts) to produce the
electromagnetic field required inside the alternator. The significance of
this is that if the battery is completely discharged (flat), the alternator will
not be able to supply any power to the electrical system, even after the
engine has been started by some other means (i.e., external power or
hand propping). Output from the alternator is controlled by a VOLTAGE
REGULATOR which is mounted behind the left hand side of the instrument panel. An OVERVOLTAGE RELAY protects the system from
possible damage due to an overvoltage condition. In the event of an overvoltage (over approximately 16.5 volts) the relay opens and it can be
assumed the alternator has failed.

The primary purposes of the BATTERY are to provide power for engine
starting, the initial excitation of the alternator, and as a backup in the
event of alternator failure. In normal operations with the engine running
the alternator provides the power to the electrical system and charges the
battery. A fully-charged battery has a charging rate of about 2 amperes; in
a partially discharged condition (i.e., just after engine start) the charging
rate can be much higher than this. In the event of an alternator failure the
battery provides *all* power to the electrical system. In theory, a fully-
charged 35-ampere-hour battery is capable of providing 35 amps for 1
hour, 1 amp for 35 hours, or 17.5 amps for 2 hours, etc. In practice, the
power available is governed by factors such as battery age and condition, load placed on it, etc. The best advice is to reduce electrical load to
the minimum consistent with safety, and plan to make a landing at the
earliest opportunity, should an electrical failure occur.

The AMMETER, located in the engine instrument group, indicates in amperes the electrical load on the alternator. With the engine running and all electrical services turned off, the ammeter will indicate the charging rate of the battery. As services are switched on the ammeter will indicate the additional load of each item. In the case of night flight, the maximum continuous load will be in the region of 30 amps. In the event of alternator failure, the ammeter will indicate zero, and where installed, a red "Low Voltage" warning light will illuminate. Except for some early Warrior I's, an ANNUNCIATOR PANEL is installed in the upper instrument panel (described in "The Oil System," page 1-15). The ALT warning light of the annunciator panel will illuminate if the alternator fails.

The pilot controls the electrical system via the MASTER SWITCH located on the instrument panel at the left end of the electrical rocker switch group. This switch is a split rocker switch having two halves, labeled BAT and ALT, and normally the switch is operated as one, both halves being used together. The BAT half of the switch can be operated independently, so that all electrical power is being drawn from the battery only; however, the ALT side can only be turned on in conjunction with the BAT half. Should an electrical problem occur, the master switch can be used to reset the electrical system by turning it OFF for 2 seconds, and then turning it ON again.

The aircraft may be fitted with an EXTERNAL POWER RECEP-TACLE at the right hand fuselage aft of the wing root, this can be

The external power receptacle.

used to connect external power for starting or operation of the aircraft electrical system. Before using external power it is imperative to check that the external power unit is of the correct voltage—otherwise *serious damage could be inflicted on the electrical system*. Additionally, it should be remembered that if the battery is totally flat (completely discharged), it will need to be removed and recharged, or replaced before flight.

To use external power the following procedure should be adopted:

1. Check that master switch and all electrical equipment are OFF.

2. Ensure that the *red* lead of the jumper cable goes to the *positive* (+) terminal of the external power source and the *black* lead to the *negative* (-).

3. Insert the cable plug into the aircraft external power receptacle socket.

4. Turn the master switch ON, and proceed with normal starting procedure.

5. After engine start, turn master switch and all electrical equipment OFF and remove the cable plug from the aircraft.

6. Turn the master switch ON, and check the ammeter. If no output is shown, flight should not be attempted.

The various electrically-operated systems are protected by individual CIRCUIT BREAKERS, which are located on the lower instrument panel. Should a problem occur (e.g., a short circuit) the relevant circuit breaker may "pop," and will be raised in relation to the other circuit breakers (CBs). The correct procedure is to allow the CB to cool for about 2 minutes, then reset it and check the result. If the CB pops again it should not be reset.

Apart from engine starting and the alternator field, the electrical system supplies power to the following:

- All internal and external lights.
- All radios and intercom.
- Turn coordinator, Fuel gauges, Oil temperature gauge, Annunciator panel.
- Stall warning, Pitot heater, Electric fuel pump.

The Stall Warning System

A horn is electrically activated from a stall warning vane on the leading edge of the left wing. This vane moves up at angles of attack approaching the stall, and gives a warning at approximately 5 to 10 knots above the stall speed.

The wing-mounted stall warning vane.

The Lighting System

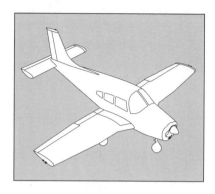

The Warrior may be equipped with a variety of optional internal and external lighting. Where wing tip "strobe" lights are installed, care should be used in their operation. As a general rule the strobes are not used during taxiing as they can dazzle and distract those nearby; they are, however, very effective in the air. If flying in cloud conditions or heavy precipitation it is recommended that they be turned off, as the pilot may become spatially disoriented. The landing light is fitted in the lower front nose cowling—again it should be used with some discretion, because of the very short life of the light bulbs.

The wing-tip navigation light and strobe light unit.

The Vacuum System

An engine-driven vacuum pump is mounted to the upper rear face of the engine. This pump is fitted with a plastic shear drive, so that should the pump seize, the shear drive will fail and the engine will not be damaged. The air enters the vacuum system through a filter, passes through the air-driven gyro instruments (and is measured by the suction gauge), into the vacuum regulator and on to the vacuum pump, from which it is expelled through a short pipe.

Suction is used to drive the gyros in the attitude indicator (or artificial horizon) and heading indicator (or direction indicator). A suction gauge mounted on the instrument panel measures suction, for cruising RPMs and altitudes the reading should be 5.0, within 0.1 inches of mercury. A lower suction over an extended period may indicate a faulty vacuum regulator, dirty screens, or a system leak. If the vacuum pump fails or a line collapses, the suction gauge reading will fall to zero, and the attitude indicator and heading indicator will become unreliable over a period of some minutes as the gyros run down, losing RPM. The real danger here is that the effect is gradual and may not be noticed by the pilot for some time.

The suction gauge.

The Pitot-Static System

The pitot-static system supplies static pressure to the vertical speed indicator (VSI) and altimeter and pitot and static pressure to the airspeed indicator (ASI).

Pitot and static pressure comes from a PITOT TUBE which is located under the left wing. No checking system is incorporated in the system, and instrument

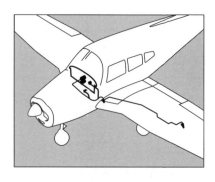

indications in the event of a leak or blockage are outside of the scope of this book. As an option, the pitot tube has a heating element which is activated by a switch in the electrical rocker switch group on the instrument panel, labeled PITOT HEAT. Pitot heat can prevent blockage of the pitot tube in heavy rain or icing. This notwithstanding, it must be remembered that *the PA-28 is not cleared for flight into known icing conditions.* Should the static lines become blocked, an alternate static source is available as an option; the control valve is located under the left instrument panel. When this valve is operated cabin air feeds the static system, the DV window and cabin vents should be closed, and the cabin heater and defrost turned on. A drain valve that serves both the pitot and static lines is located on the lower left cabin wall.

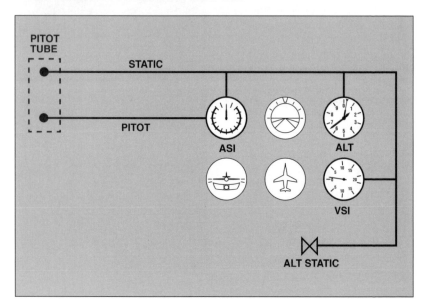

The pitot tube.

The pitot tube should be checked before flight to ensure that the pitot and static ports are unobstructed. The pitot tube may be protected on the ground with a removable pitot cover. It is important not to blow into either pitot or static vents; doing so can result in damage to the pressure instruments.

The Heating and Ventilation System

Cabin heating is supplied by a shroud around the engine exhaust system. This allows air, which has entered from an inlet in the rear engine baffles inside the cowling, to be warmed by the exhaust pipes. It can then be directed to outlets between the front seats (cabin heat) or at the lower windscreen (defrost) by two levers mounted at the far right instrument panel. The system is very effective once the engine is warm, although its use is governed by a couple of safety factors.

First, the heating system effectively opens a path through the firewall between the engine compartment and the cockpit. For this reason the cabin heat and defrost are selected OFF before engine start, or if fire is suspected in the engine compartment.

Second, with a system of this type there is a danger of carbon monoxide (CO) being introduced into the cabin. Carbon monoxide is a gas produced as a by-product of the combustion process. It is colorless, odorless and tasteless, but its effects are potentially fatal. The dangers of carbon monoxide are widely publicized. A generally accepted practice is to shut off the heating system if engine fumes (which may contain CO) are thought to be entering the cockpit. The danger arises if a crack or split is present in the exhaust system inside the heating shroud, allowing carbon monoxide to enter the heating system.

The ventilation system consists of cockpit vents, individually controlled, directing fresh air to just ahead of each seat. The inlets for this air are in the inner leading edge of each wing. In addition, an overhead ventilation system may be fitted. This system takes fresh air from an inlet in the leading edge of the fin to vents in the cabin ceiling. An electrically powered blower may be fitted to the overhead ventilation system to boost air

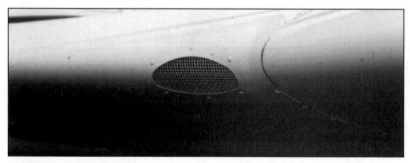

The leading edge fresh air vent.

through this system when on the ground. When the heating system is in use it is recommended that you operate the fresh air vents to give a comfortable temperature mix. Doing so will help to combat the possible danger of carbon monoxide poisoning, and will prevent the cabin from becoming "stuffy" and possibly inducing drowsiness.

Seats and Harnesses

The front seats are adjustable fore and aft. The bar which unlocks the seat position is located below the forward edge of the seat cushion. This bar is raised and then the seat can be moved fore and aft. When the desired position is reached, the bar is released and the pilot should check that the seat is positively locked in position. As an option, the front seats may also be adjustable for height. Generally, entry to and exit from the front seats is easiest with the seats in the rearmost position. When the seats are unoccupied, the seat backs can be tilted forward to allow access to the rear seats. To get to the rear seats, the front seats are best in the full forward position. The Cadet may have a rear "bench" seat fitted as an option.

Harness design may vary between different aircraft. In addition to the lap strap, a single inertia reel shoulder strap is fitted and their use should be considered mandatory. Upper torso restraint has been shown to be a major factor in accident survivability. The inertia reel can be checked by pulling sharply on the shoulder strap; the reel should lock and prevent the strap from extending further.

The baggage area behind the rear seats is fitted with restraint straps for the securing of items placed in this area. For the Warrior and Archer, maximum baggage to be carried in this area is 200 lbs, evenly distributed. For the Cadet the maximum baggage is 50 lbs. Attention should be drawn to the weight and balance implications of weight in this area. It also must be remembered that for some maneuvers, carrying baggage is prohibited.

Doors and Windows

The PA-28 has a single door on the right hand side of the cabin to allow for access to the cabin via the right wing walkway.

The design of the door latches varies according to the model year of the particular aircraft. On Warriors pre-1976, the cabin door has a simple "pull to open" latch ahead of the door armrest. This is supplemented by a latch on the upper portion of the door. From inside, the lever is rotated rear-wards to latch the door; the inward movement of the upper part of the door normally makes it clear that the latch has engaged. On 1976 models and on, the overhead latch operates in the same fashion, but the latch in front of the door armrest must, in addition, be moved down in order to latch the door completely.

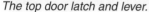

The top door latch and lever.

The lower door locking lever.

Although it is important for the door to be properly latched for flight, the consequences of partial door opening in flight are usually not serious. In fact the door can usually be closed by slowing to about 87 knots IAS, with the DV window open and the cabin vents closed. The offending latch can then be operated, while pulling on the door if necessary.

Where accidents do occur after a door opens in-flight, they are often caused by pilot distraction from the primary task of flying the airplane, rather than as a direct result of the open door.

When entering and leaving the cabin, the top of the door should not be used as a hand grip to support body weight, as damage to the door and door hinges may result.

The rear baggage door.

A separate BAGGAGE DOOR is fitted to the right side of the Warrior and Archer models (but not the Cadet) to allow easy access to the baggage area. It is important to check that this door is properly closed and latched before flight.

An inward-opening DV WINDOW is fitted to the left hand window. This window can be opened in flight where visibility through the windscreen has been impaired, or to aid ventilation.

The aircraft design and window area gives the aircraft reasonable forward and side visibility. This visibility can be degraded by oil smears, insects and other matter accumulating on the windows. For window cleaning, a soft cloth and warm soapy water are recommended; to remove oil and grease a cloth soaked in kerosene can be used. The use of gasoline, alcohol, thinners and window cleaner sprays is not recommended.

The DV window.

Section 2
Limitations

PA-28-161 Warrior and PA-28-181 Archer Dimensions

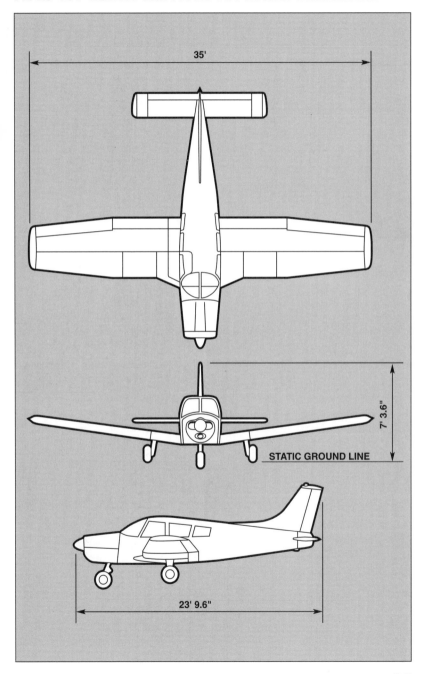

PA-28-161 Cadet Dimensions

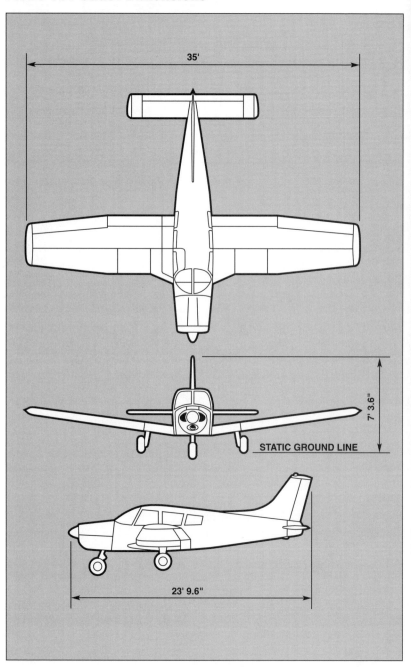

The "V" Airspeed Code

V_{S0} – (Low end of white arc) Stalling speed with full flaps.

V_{S1} – (Low end of green arc) Stalling speed without flaps.

V_{FE} – Maximum airspeed with flaps extended. Do not extend flaps above this speed, or fly faster than this speed with any flaps extended.

V_A – Design maneuvering speed. Do not make full or abrupt control movements when flying faster than this speed. Design maneuvering speed should not be exceeded when flying in turbulent conditions.

V_{NO} – Maximum structural cruising speed. Do not exceed this speed except in smooth air conditions.

V_{NE} – Never exceed speed. Do not exceed this airspeed under any circumstances.

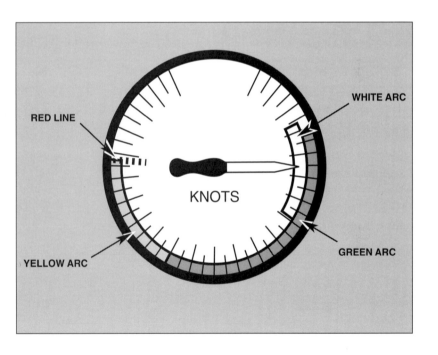

PA-28-161 Warrior II Limitations

Airspeed Limitations PA-28-161 (Warrior II)
(all quoted speeds are INDICATED airspeed—IAS)

	Knots	MPH
V_{NE}	160	184
V_{NO}	126	145
V_A (at 2240 lbs)	111	128
V_A (at 1531 lbs)	88	101
V_{FE}	103	118
Stalling Speed clean	50	58
Stalling Speed Full Flaps	44	51

Airspeed Indicator Markings PA-28-161 (Warrior II)

	Knots	MPH
RED LINE (Never Exceed)	160	184
YELLOW ARC (Caution range)	126 – 160	145 – 184
GREEN ARC (Normal operating range)	50 – 126	58 – 145
WHITE ARC (Flaps extended range)	44 – 103	51 – 118

Maximum Demonstrated
Crosswind Component PA-28-161 (Warrior II)   17 Knots

Airframe Limitations PA-28-161 (Warrior II)

Weights	Normal	Utility
Maximum Takeoff Weight	2440 lbs	2020 lbs
Maximum Landing Weight	2440 lbs	2020 lbs
Maximum Baggage Weight	200 lbs	0

Flight Load Factors PA-28-161 (Warrior II)

	Normal	Utility
Max. Positive load factor:	3.8G	4.4G

Max. Negative load factor: *No Inverted Maneuvers Permitted*

Miscellaneous Limitations PA-28-161 (Warrior II)

Nose Wheel Tire Pressure	30 psi
Main Wheel Tire Pressure	24 psi

PA-28-161 Cadet Limitations

Airspeed Limitations PA-28-161 (Cadet)
(quoted speeds are INDICATED airspeed—IAS)

	Knots	MPH
V_{NE}	160	184
V_{NO}	126	145
V_A (at 2325 lbs)	111	128
V_A (at 1531 lbs)	88	101
V_{FE}	103	118
Stalling Speed clean	50	58
Stalling Speed Full Flaps	44	51

Airspeed Indicator Markings PA-28-161 (Cadet)

	Knots	MPH
RED LINE (Never Exceed)	160	184
YELLOW ARC (Caution range)	126 – 160	145 – 184
GREEN ARC (Normal operating range)	50 – 126	58 – 145
WHITE ARC (Flaps extended range)	44 – 103	51 – 118

**Maximum Demonstrated
Crosswind Component** PA-28-161 (Cadet)   17 Knots

Airframe Limitations PA-28-161 (Cadet)

Weights	Normal	Utility
Maximum Takeoff Weight	2325 lbs	2020 lbs
Maximum Landing Weight	2325 lbs	2020 lbs
Maximum Baggage Weight	50 lbs	0

Flight Load Factors PA-28-161 (Cadet)

	Normal	Utility
Max. Positive load factor:	3.8G	4.4G

Max. Negative load factor: *No Inverted Maneuvers Permitted*

Miscellaneous Limitations PA-28-161 (Cadet)

Nose Wheel Tire Pressure	30 psi
Main Wheel Tire Pressure	24 psi

PA-28-181 Archer II Limitations

Airspeed Limitations PA-28-181 (Archer II)
(all quoted speeds are INDICATED airspeed—IAS)

	Knots	MPH
V_{NE}	154	177
V_{NO}	125	144
V_A (at 2550 lbs)	113	130
V_A (at 1634 lbs)	89	102
V_{FE}	102	117
Stalling Speed clean	55	63
Stalling Speed Full Flaps	49	56

Airspeed Indicator Markings PA-28-181 (Archer II)

	Knots	MPH
RED LINE (Never Exceed)	154	177
YELLOW ARC (Caution range)	125 – 154	144 – 177
GREEN ARC (Normal operating range)	55 – 125	63 – 144
WHITE ARC (Flaps extended range)	49 – 102	56 – 117

Maximum Demonstrated
Crosswind Component PA-28-181 (Archer II)   17 Knots

Airframe Limitations PA-28-181 (Archer II)

Weights	Normal	Utility
Maximum Takeoff Weight	2550 lbs	2130 lbs
Maximum Landing Weight	2550 lbs	2130 lbs
Maximum Baggage Weight	200 lbs	0

Flight Load Factors PA-28-181 (Archer II)

	Normal	Utility
Max. Positive load factor:	3.8G	4.4G

Max. Negative load factor: *No Inverted Maneuvers Permitted*

Miscellaneous Limitations PA-28-181 (Archer II)

Nose Wheel Tire Pressure	18 psi
Main Wheel Tire Pressure	24 psi

PA-28 Limitations
Engine Limitations

	Tachometer	Instrument Marking
Maximum RPM	2700	Red Line
Normal Operating Range	500 – 2700	Green Arc
	Oil Temperature	**Instrument Marking**
Normal operating range	75 – 245°F	Green Arc
Maximum	245°F	Red Line
	Oil Pressure	**Instrument Marking**
Normal operating range	60 – 90 psi	Green Arc
Minimum	25 psi	Red Line
Maximum	100 psi (1)	Red Line
Caution range—idle	25 – 60 psi	Yellow Arc
Caution range—warm up (2)	90 – 100 psi	Yellow Arc

(1) 90 psi for Archer II
(2) Warrior II only

Oil Quantity

	US quart
Capacity	8
Minimum safe quantity	2
	(+1 quart per hour planned flight)

Fuel System

Fuel Quantity

	US Gal
Total Capacity	50
Unusable Fuel	2
Usable Fuel	48
Indicator Tab	34 (17 per tank)

Fuel Pressure		Gauge Indication
Maximum	8.0 psi	Red Line
Minimum	0.5 psi	Red Line
Normal operating range	0.5 – 8.0 psi	Green Arc

Oil Grades

Lycoming approves lubricating oil for the engine that conforms to specification MIL-L-6082 (straight mineral type) and specification MIL-L-22851 (ashless dispersant type).

Straight mineral oil is usually only used when the engine is new, or after maintenance work on the engine. Straight oil grades are known by their weight.

Ashless dispersant oils are more commonly used in service. This oil must not be used when the engine is operating on straight mineral oil. It is therefore very important to check which type of oil is currently being used in the engine, and be sure only to add the same type.

Both types of oil are available in different grades, used according to the average surface air temperature. The recommended grades are set out as SAE numbers. The table below shows the recommended grades for various temperature bands.

AVERAGE SURFACE AIR TEMPERATURE	MIL-L-6082 Straight mineral
Above 60°F / 16°C	SAE 50
30°F / -1°C – 90°F / 32°C	SAE 40
0°F / -18°C – 70°F / 21°C	SAE 30
Below 10°F / -12°C	SAE 20
AVERAGE SURFACE AIR TEMPERATURE	MIL-L-22851 Ashless Dispersant
Above 60°F / 16°C	SAE 50 or SAE 40
30°F / -1°C – 90°F / 32°C	SAE 40
0°F / -18°C – 70°F / 21°C	SAE 30 or SAE 40
Below 10°F / -12°C	SAE 30

Fuel Grades

The PA-28 Warrior is certified for use with 100LL fuels.

The table below shows the recommended fuel grades. It is wise to pay attention when your aircraft is being refueled, especially if at an airfield new to you. More than one pilot has found out that piston engines designed for AVGAS do not run very well on turbine fuel (Jet A-1). To help guard against this eventuality AVGAS fueling points carry a RED sticker, and turbine fuel fueling points a BLACK sticker.

APPROVED FUEL GRADES
100LL
100L
100

Section 3
Handling the PA-28 Warrior

Engine Starting

Starting the Warrior is straightforward, but the ambient conditions and engine temperature are the prime factors to be considered. A cold engine will require between 2 and 4 primes; a hot engine should not require any

priming at all. The throttle is set to one-quarter open (that is, 1/4-inch in), with the mixture rich and fuel set to the tank with the lowest quantity (unless of course that tank is empty).

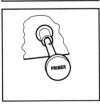

Cranking the starter should be limited to 30 seconds at a time, due to the danger of the starter motor overheating. After a prolonged period of engine cranking without a successful start the starter should be allowed a few minutes to cool before a further attempt is made. The starter should not be operated after engine start, because damage to the starter may result.

"Pumping" of the throttle during starting should be avoided, as it can lead to an engine fire on start.

After start, the oil pressure should register within 30 seconds. If the oil pressure does not register, the engine should be shut down without delay. Readings on the suction gauge and ammeter are also usually checked after engine start.

Starting With a Suspected Flooded Engine

An over-primed (flooded) engine will be indicated by weak intermittent firing, and puffs of black smoke from the exhaust during the attempted start. If it is suspected that the engine is flooded (over-primed) the throttle should be opened full and the mixture moved to idle cut-off. If the engine starts, the throttle should be retarded to the normal position and the mixture moved to full rich.

Starting In Cold Ambient Conditions (below 0°C)

Failure to start due to an under-primed engine is more likely to occur in cold conditions with a cold engine. An under-primed engine will not fire at all, and additional priming is necessary. Starting in cold temperatures will be more difficult due to a number of factors. The oil will be more viscous, the battery may lose up to half of its capacity and the fuel will not vaporize readily. A greater number of primes will be required, external power may be needed to supplement the aircraft battery, and pre-heat may be necessary in very low temperatures.

Taxiing

In the first few feet of taxiing a brake check is normally carried out, followed by steering and differential brake checks in due course. It is common practice to check the hand operated brake lever in addition to the toe brakes (if these are installed). The direct link, via steering rods, from the rudder pedals to the nose wheel makes the Warrior easy to steer accurately, although on earlier models the steering is quite heavy to operate. Use of differential brakes can give a very small turning circle, although increased power is often required when using prolonged differential braking. Where toe brakes are not installed, the brake lever can be used in conjunction with full rudder to reduce turn radius. When taxiing with a crosswind, "opposite rudder" will be required, up to full deflection; e.g., with a crosswind from the left, up to full right rudder may be required as the aircraft tries to "weathervane" into the wind. In this situation differential braking will also aid directional control.

The figure below shows recommended control column positions when taxiing with the prevailing wind from the directions shown.

Speed control is important, especially when taxiing over rough surfaces or in strong wind conditions. When slowing the aircraft, the throttle should always be closed first, and then the brakes evenly applied to slow the aircraft.

During ground operations care should be taken to avoid prolonged idling of the engine, as this may result in fouled spark plugs.

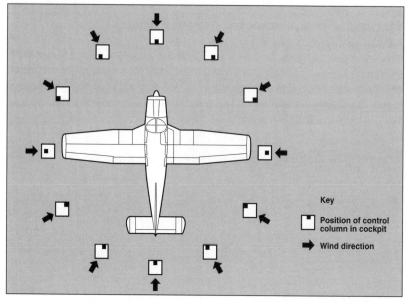

Key

■ Position of control column in cockpit

➡ Wind direction

Power And Pre-Takeoff Checks

The aircraft is usually positioned into the wind to aid engine cooling, and before the power checks start, the oil temperature should be in the green arc.

The engine is generally run up to 2,000 RPM, with the fuel tank with greatest quantity selected (the same tank should be used for takeoff). At this RPM the carburetor heat is checked, and a small drop in RPM should be noted. The subject of carburetor icing is covered in Section 4; however, an important point to note is that the inlet for the "hot" air is unfiltered. Therefore dust, grass, etc., may well enter the engine when "hot" air is selected, leading to increased engine wear. For this reason the use of carburetor heat should be kept to the minimum necessary while on the ground.

The magnetos are checked individually, with no more than 3 seconds on each magneto recommended to avoid spark plug fouling. A small drop in RPM is the norm and shows that the ignition system is functioning properly. No RPM drop at all when operating on one magneto may well indicate a malfunction in the ignition system, and the possibility that one or both magnetos are staying "live." An excessive drop in RPM when operating on one magneto, especially when accompanied by rough running, may indicate fouled spark plugs or a faulty magneto. If fouled plugs are suspected it may be possible for the pilot to clear the problem. The engine is set to about 2,000 RPM with magnetos on BOTH, and the mixture leaned to give the "peak" RPM. This should be held for about 10 seconds; then the mixture is returned to full rich, and the magnetos can be rechecked.

WARNING: Excessive power setting and over-lean mixture settings should be avoided during this procedure. If the problem does not clear, the aircraft should be considered unfit to fly.

The engine gauges, together with the suction gauge and ammeter, are checked at 2,000 RPM for normal indications.

Takeoff

Normally, takeoff is made with the mixture in the full RICH position. At high elevation airfields (above about 3,000 feet MSL) it may be necessary to lean the mixture before takeoff to give maximum power.

For all takeoffs care must be taken to ensure that the feet remain clear of the toe brakes (where these are fitted), this is best done by keeping your heels on the floor. It should also be positively confirmed that the brake lever is fully OFF.

At the start of the takeoff run (as at all other times), the throttle should be opened smoothly and progressively—rapid opening of the throttle should be specifically avoided. The normal rotation speed is 50 knots, with a climb speed of 80 knots dependent on conditions and operator procedures. In crosswind conditions, the rotation speed should be increased to ensure full control immediately after takeoff. For "short field" takeoffs the use of 2 stages of flaps (25°) is common practice, with a slower climb-out speed.

On rough surfaces particularly, it is important to protect the nose wheel by keeping weight off it during the takeoff run; although "over-rotating" should be avoided as this will lengthen the takeoff run—and ruin the view ahead!

Climbing

An airspeed in the region of 79 knots will give the best rate of climb after takeoff. The best angle of climb (the best increase in height for the shortest distance traveled over the ground), can be obtained at about 63 knots. During climbing it is important to monitor the engine gauges, as the engine is operating at a high power setting but with a reduced cooling airflow compared to cruising flight. Lookout ahead is impaired by the high nose attitude, and it is common practice to "weave" the nose periodically during the climb to visually check the area ahead.

Cruising Flight

Cruising is normally done with a power setting of 55–75%. Typically a setting of 2,200 RPM will give an indicated airspeed of around 105 knots for the Warrior. If turbulent conditions are encountered in flight, particular care must be taken not to exceed the V_A (Design Maneuvering Speed). The V_A for a PA-28-161 Warrior is 111 knots, reducing as weight is reduced.

Engine Handling

Engine rough running can be caused by a number of factors. It should be remembered that the majority of engine failures in light aircraft are due to pilot error. After carburetor icing, fuel exhaustion (running out of fuel) or fuel starvation (i.e., fuel on-board but not reaching the engine) are common causes of engine failure. Having sufficient fuel on board to complete the flight is a point of basic airmanship, and mostly accomplished through proper flight planning and thorough pre-flight checks. Keeping the fuel tanks in balance and monitoring the fuel system are a part of the cruise checks. When the fuel tanks are changed in flight the electric fuel pump should be turned on before the change, and left on until about 30 seconds after the change. Fuel starvation may occur if the engine driven fuel pump fails. In this instance the use of the electric fuel pump should restore the fuel supply to the engine and allow for a diversion to be made.

Regular monitoring of the engine instruments may forewarn of an impending problem. High oil temperature may indicate a faulty gauge, if not accompanied by a corresponding drop in oil pressure. As with most instances, the action to be taken will depend on the pilot's judgment of the situation at the time. A reasonable course of action would be a diversion to a suitable airfield, while remaining alert to the possibility of a sudden engine failure.

Where high oil temperature is accompanied by a low oil pressure, engine failure may very well be imminent, and the pilot should act accordingly. Such a situation might occur during a prolonged slow climb in hot conditions. In this instance, increasing the airspeed to provide more cooling, and reducing power if possible, may restore oil temperature to normal. In the event of a low oil pressure reading, accompanied by a normal oil temperature reading, gauge failure may be the culprit, and the pilot can consider actions similar to those for an oil temperature gauge failure.

Stalling

A Reminder: The information in this section is no substitute for flight instruction under the guidance of a flight instructor familiar with the aircraft and its characteristics.

The aircraft is generally straightforward in its stalling behavior. The stall warning horn activates 5 to 10 knots above the stall airspeed. Because it is electrically operated, the stall warning is inoperative with the master switch off, or with a faulty electrical system. The actual stall speed can be affected by many factors, including the aircraft weight and center of gravity position. The use of power will lower the stalling speed, while turning flight raises the stall speed. The use of flaps, power, or turning flight considerably increases the chance of a wing drop at the stall. When practicing stalls the possibility of a wing drop can be reduced by keeping the aircraft coordinated during the approach to the stall. Typical height loss for a full stall with a conventional recovery (using power) is about 200 feet. A gentle stall and absence of wing drop characterize the Warrior stall; the stall is preceded by mild airframe buffeting and gentle pitching.

In-service experience has shown that the aircraft may roll sharply to the right while stalling with high power settings and aft CG positions. To cure this problem a temporary aft CG position restriction was introduced, while leading edge stall strips are fitted to the wing. Check the status of the aircraft if planning to practice stalling.

Spins

The Warrior, Cadet and Archer *are not cleared* for intentional spinning. Should an inadvertent spin occur, the recommended spin recovery is:

- Check ailerons neutral and throttle idle.
- Apply and maintain full opposite rudder (opposite to the direction of spin).
- Move the control wheel full forward.
- When rotation stops center the rudder and recover from the ensuing dive.

Descent

The descent may be powered or glide. For the glide, a speed of about 70 knots is standard. Where flaps are used the rate of descent increases. The initial lowering of flaps leads to a definite nose-up pitching and reduced airspeed. The low power settings usually used during the descent, and a possible prolonged descent into warmer air, provide ideal conditions for carburetor icing; full carburetor heat should be used where necessary. In a glide descent, power should be added for short periods throughout the descent to help prevent plug fouling, rapid cylinder cooling, and of course, carburetor icing.

Landing

For the approach to landing the mixture should be full RICH (unless landing at a very high elevation airfield), the electric fuel pump should be on and the fuel tank with the greatest quantity selected. The aircraft is not difficult to land; however, in common with most light aircraft, care should be taken to protect the nose wheel.

The nose wheel is nowhere near as strong as the main gear, but there is no need for its strength to be tested if a proper approach and landing technique are used. Approach speed for a normal approach with flaps is about 70 knots, usually a little higher for a flapless approach. Incorrect approach speed is a primary cause of "ballooning," which often leads to bouncing. Bouncing also occurs where the aircraft is allowed to touch down at too high a speed, usually in a level attitude rather than a nose up attitude. The correct action in either a "balloon" or a bounce is to GO AROUND without delay. The correct landing technique is to approach at the proper speed, "flare" or "hold off" for landing, close the throttle, and gradually raise the nose to ensure a slow touch down speed on the *mainwheels first,* with the nose wheel still off the ground. As the aircraft slows down, correct use of the stabilator means the nose wheel is allowed to gently contact the surface some time after the initial mainwheel contact. Again, there is no substitute for flight instruction in the proper technique with a flight instructor.

The go-around does not pose any particular problems, even with full flaps extended. The trim change when applying full power is manageable, and although the aircraft will climb with full flaps extended, it is common practice to raise flaps to the second stage (25°) as part of the immediate go-around actions. During the go-around, as at all other times, the throttle should be opened smoothly, from idle to full throttle in not less than 2 seconds. This is done specifically to avoid the accelerator pump causing an over-rich mixture and consequent loss of power.

Parking and Tie Down

The aircraft is generally parked into the wind; it is good practice to stop with the nose wheel straight so that the rudder is not deflected. All switches should be off, and the doors closed. In extremely cold weather it may be advisable *not* to set the parking brake as moisture may freeze the brakes. In addition the parking brake should not be set if there is reason to believe that the brakes are overheated. If for any reason the parking brake is not set the wheels should be "chocked."

When tying down the aircraft the following technique is recommended:

- Park the aircraft into the wind with the flaps retracted.

- Secure the flight controls by looping the seat belt through the control wheel.

- Tie ropes, cables or chains to the wing tie-down points and secure them to ground anchor points with the ropes, etc., at approximately 45° to the ground.

- If desired, a rope (not cable or chain) can be secured to the nose gear and secured to a ground anchor point.

- A rope can be passed through the tail tie-down point and each end secured at a 45° angle to the ground each side of the tail.

- External control locks may be advisable in strong or gusty wind conditions.

It is also prudent to use a pitot cover, particularly if the aircraft will be left unattended for some time.

Section 4
Mixture and Carburetor Icing Supplement

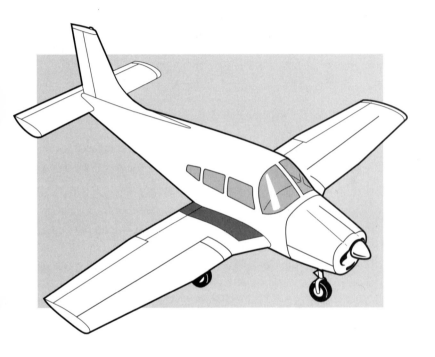

Carburetor Icing

Almost certainly the most common cause of engine rough-running, and complete engine failure, is carburetor icing. Despite this, carburetor icing remains a widely misunderstood subject. Many pilots' knowledge of the subject is limited to a feeling that the carburetor heat should be used regularly in flight, without really knowing the symptoms of carburetor icing or the conditions most likely to cause its formation.

How Carburetor Icing Forms

IMPACT ICING occurs when ice forms over the external air inlet (air filter) and inside the induction system leading to the carburetor. This type of icing occurs with the temperature below 0°C while flying in clouds, or in precipitation (i.e., rain, sleet or snow). These conditions are also conducive to airframe icing, and the aircraft is *not cleared for flight into known icing conditions,* which clearly these are. So, assuming the aircraft is operated legally within its limitations, this form of icing should not occur, and is not considered further.

CARBURETOR ICING is caused by a temperature drop inside the carburetor, which can happen even in conditions where other forms of icing will not occur. The causes of this temperature drop are twofold:

1. FUEL ICING—the evaporation of fuel inside the carburetor. Liquid fuel changes to fuel vapor and mixes with the induction air causing a large temperature drop. If the temperature inside the carburetor falls below 0°C, water vapor in the atmosphere condenses into ice, usually on the walls of the carburetor passage adjacent to the fuel jet, and on the throttle valve. Generally, fuel icing is responsible for around 70% of the temperature drop in the carburetor.

2. THROTTLE ICING—the temperature loss caused by the acceleration of air and consequent pressure drop around the throttle valve. This effect may again take the temperature below 0°C, and water vapor in the inlet air will condense into ice on the throttle valve. This practical effect is a demonstration of Bernoulli's Principle.

As fuel and throttle icing generally occur together, they are known just as carburetor icing.

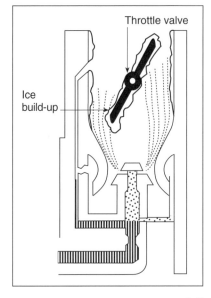

Throttle valve

Ice build-up

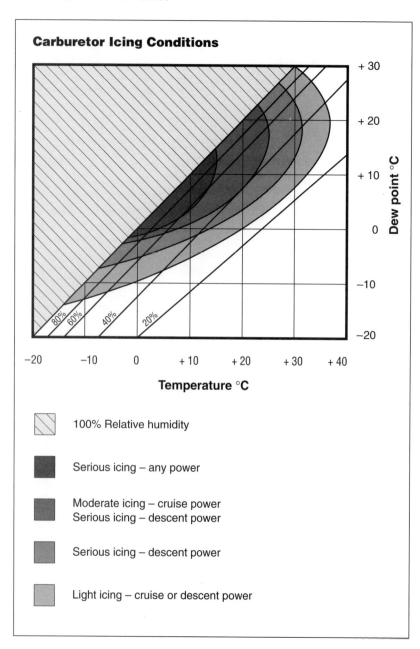

Conditions Likely to Lead to Carburetor Icing

Two criteria govern the likelihood of carburetor icing conditions: the AIR TEMPERATURE and the RELATIVE HUMIDITY.

The ambient air temperature is important, *but not because the tempera-ture needs to be below 0°C, or even close to freezing.* The temperature drop in the carburetor can be up to 30°C, so carburetor icing can (and does) occur in hot ambient conditions. It is no wonder carburetor icing is sometimes referred to as refrigeration icing. Carburetor icing is consid-ered a possibility within the temperature range of -10°C to +30°C.

The relative humidity (a measure of the water content of the atmosphere) is a major factor. The greater the water content in the atmosphere (the higher the relative humidity), the greater the risk of carburetor icing. That said, the relative humidity (RH) does not to have to be 100% (i.e., visible water droplets—cloud, rain), for carburetor icing to occur. Carburetor icing is considered a possibility at relative humidity values as low as 30%. Herein lies perhaps the real danger of carburetor icing, that it can occur in such a wide range of conditions. Obviously the pilot must be alert to the possibility of carburetor icing at just about all times. Flight in or near clouds, or in other visible moisture (i.e., rain) might be an obvious cause of carburetor icing, but—*visible moisture does not need to be present for carburetor icing to occur.*

Symptoms of Carburetor Icing

In this aircraft, fitted with a fixed pitch propeller, the symptoms of carbure-tor icing are straightforward. A loss of RPM will be the first symptom, although this is often first noticed as a loss of altitude. As the icing becomes more serious, engine rough-running may occur.

Carburetor icing is often detected during the use of the carburetor heat. Normally when the carburetor heat is used, a small drop in RPM occurs; when the control is returned to cold (off) the RPM restores to the same as before the use of carburetor heat. If the RPM restores to a figure higher than before the carburetor heat was used, it can be assumed that some form of carburetor icing was present.

Use of Carburetor Heat

Apart from the normal check of carburetor heat during the power checks, it may be necessary to use the carburetor heat on the ground if carburetor icing is suspected. Safety considerations apart, the use of carburetor heat on the ground should be kept to a minimum, because the hot air inlet is unfiltered and sand or dust can enter the engine, increasing engine wear.

Carburetor icing is generally considered to be very unlikely with the engine operating at above 75% power, i.e., during the takeoff and climb. Carburetor heat should not be used with the engine operating at above 75% power (i.e., full throttle) as detonation may occur. Detonation is the uncontrolled burning of fuel in the cylinders, literally an explosion, and will cause serious damage to the engine very quickly. Apart from the danger of detonation, the use of carburetor heat reduces the power the engine produces. In any situation where full power is required (i.e., takeoff, climb, go-around) the carburetor heat must be off (cold).

Very few operators recommend the use of anything other than FULL carburetor heat. A normal carburetor icing check will involve leaving the carburetor heat on (hot) for 5 to 10 seconds, although the pilot may wish to vary this dependent on the conditions. The use of carburetor heat does increase the fuel consumption, and this may be a factor to consider if the aircraft is being flown towards the limit of its range/endurance in possible carburetor icing conditions.

With carburetor icing present, the use of carburetor heat may lead to a large drop in RPM, with rough running. The instinctive reaction is to put the carburetor heat back to cold (off), and quickly—this is, however, the wrong action. Chances are this rough running is a good thing, and the carburetor heat should be left on (hot) until the rough running clears, and the RPM rises. In this instance, the use of carburetor heat has melted a large amount of accumulated icing, and the melted ice is passing through the engine causing temporary rough running.

Care should be taken when flying in very cold ambient conditions (below -10°C). In these conditions the use of carburetor heat may actually raise

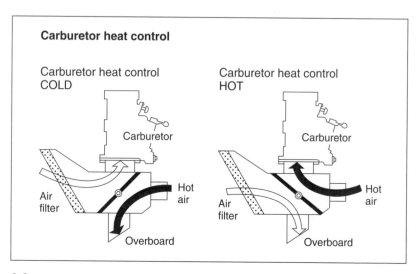

Carburetor heat control

Carburetor heat control COLD

Carburetor

Air filter

Hot air

Overboard

Carburetor heat control HOT

Carburetor

Air filter

Hot air

Overboard

the temperature in the carburetor to that most conducive to carburetor icing. Generally, when the temperature in the carburetor is below -8°C, moisture forms directly into ice crystals which pass through the engine.

The RPM loss normally associated with the use of carburetor heat is caused by the reduced density of the hot air entering the carburetor, leading to an over-rich mixture entering the engine. If the carburetor heat has to be left constantly on (hot)—i.e., flight in heavy rain and clouds—it may be advisable to lean the mixture in order to maintain RPM and smooth engine running.

It is during the descent (and particularly the glide descent) that carburetor icing is most likely to occur. The position of the throttle valve (i.e., almost closed) is a contributory factor, and even though the carburetor heat is normally applied throughout a glide descent, the low engine power will reduce the temperature of the hot air selected with the carburetor heat control. In addition, a loss of power may not be readily noticed, as the propeller is likely to windmill even after a complete loss of power. A full loss of power may only be apparent when the throttle is opened at the bottom of the descent. This is one good reason for opening the throttle to "clear the engine" at intervals during a glide descent.

The Mixture Control

The aircraft is provided with a mixture control, so that the pilot can adjust the fuel/air mixture entering the engine when necessary. The cockpit mixture control operates a needle valve between the float bowl and the main metering jet. This valve controls the fuel flow to the main metering jet to adjust the mixture. With the mixture control in the idle cut-off position (full lean), the valve is fully closed.

Reasons for Adjusting the Mixture

Correct leaning of the engine will enable the engine to be operated at its most efficient in terms of fuel consumption. With the increased use of 100LL fuel, leaning is also important to reduce spark plug fouling.

The most efficient engine operation is obtained with a fuel/air ratio of about 1:15; that is, 1 part fuel to 15 parts air. In fact, with the mixture set to full rich, the system is designed to give a slightly richer mixture than ideal; typically about 1:12. This slightly over-rich mixture reduces the possibility of pre-ignition or detonation, and aids cylinder cooling.

Effects of Mixture Adjustment

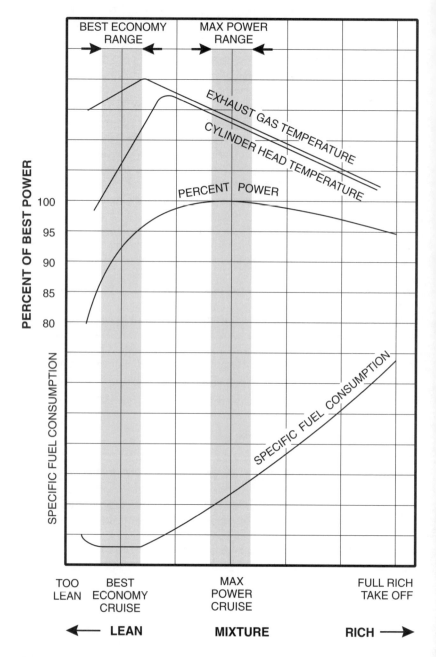

As altitude increases, the air density decreases. Above about 3,000 feet the reduced air density can lead to an over-rich mixture. If the mixture becomes excessively rich, power will be lost, rough running may be evident and ultimately engine failure will occur due to a "rich out." It is for this reason that the mixture control is provided to ensure the correct fuel/air ratio; typically it is used when cruising above 3,000 feet.

The flight manuals for some older aircraft recommend leaning only above 5,000 feet. However, with the increasing use of AVGAS 100LL, and the plug fouling problems sometimes associated with 100LL, most operators recommend leaning once above 3,000 feet.

Use of the Mixture Control

For takeoff and climb, the mixture should be full rich; the only exception is operation from a high density altitude airport, when leaning may be necessary to ensure the availability of maximum power. On reaching a cruising altitude above about 3,000 feet, the cruise power should be set, and then leaning can be carried out. (Note: Generally, leaning with over 75% power set is not recommended.) If climbing above about 5,000 feet, full throttle will be less than 75% power on a normally aspirated engine, and so leaning may be permissible to maintain smooth running.

Assuming that there is no Exhaust Gas Temperature (EGT) gauge and no cylinder head temperature gauge, the primary instrument to watch when leaning is the RPM gauge (tachometer).

To lean the engine, the recommended power setting (RPM) is set with the throttle. Next, with a constant throttle setting, the mixture control is slowly moved back (leaned). If leaning is required, the RPM will increase slowly, peak, and then decrease as the mixture is leaned. If leaning is continued, the engine will ultimately run rough and lose power.

If the mixture is set to achieve peak RPM, the maximum power mixture has been achieved.

If the mixture is set to give a tachometer reading 25 to 50 RPM less than peak RPM on the "lean" side, the best economy mixture has been achieved. This setting is the one that many aircraft manufacturers recommend, and their performance claims are based on such a procedure.

Using a mixture that is too lean is a false economy, and will lead to serious engine damage sooner or later. Detonation (an uncontrolled explosive combustion of the mixture in the cylinder) is particularly danger-ous, and can lead to an engine failure in a very short time. The use of a full rich mixture during full power operations is specifically to ensure engine cooling and guard against detonation.

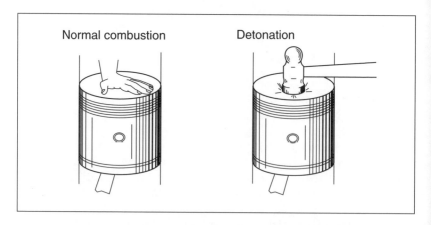

Normal combustion   Detonation

For any change in operating conditions (altitude, power setting) the mixture will need to be reset. It is particularly important that the mixture is set to full rich before increasing the power setting.

During a descent from a high altitude, the mixture will gradually become too lean if not enriched, leading to excessive cylinder temperatures, power loss and ultimately engine failure. Normally the mixture is set to full rich prior to landing, unless operating at a high elevation airfield.

Moving the mixture to the full lean position—ICO (idle cut-off)—closes the needle valve, and so stops fuel supply to the main metering jet. This is the normal method for shutting down the engine and ensures that no unburned fuel mixture is left in the engine.

Section 5
Expanded PA-28
Pre-Flight Checklist

Approaching Aircraft

1. Check for and remove any tie-downs, external control locks, pitot cover and wheel chocks.

2. Look for any oil and fuel spillage from aircraft.

3. Remove any ice and frost from *all* surfaces.

4. Check for access to taxiways, obstructions, loose gravel, etc.

5. Look to see if aircraft is on a level surface. This may effect the visual check of fuel quantity.

In Cabin

1. **Internal Control Locks and Covers** .... Remove, stow securely.

2. **Parking Brake** .... Check ON with locking plate in.

3. **Magneto Switches** .... Check OFF and key out.

4. **Master Switch** .... On.
   Turn on Pitot heater, anti-collision beacon, landing light and navigation lights. Leave cockpit and check:

5. **Stall Warning Vane** .... Move gently forward to check.

6. **Pitot Heat** .... Check with fingers that pitot tube is warm (it may take a minute or so to warm up).

7. **Anti-Collision Beacon** .... Check operation (rotating red light on tail).

8. **Landing/Nav lights** .... Check. Navigation lights colors are: PORT (Left) – Red; STARBOARD (Right) – Green; REAR (Tail) – White
   Return to cockpit and turn off electrical services.

9. **Fuel** .... Turn ON—check quantity gauges.

10. **Master Switch** .... Off.

11. **Flaps** .... Lower to second stage (25°).

12. **Trim tab** .... Check position neutral using indicator.

13. **First Aid Kit** .... Check in position, secure.

14. **Fire Extinguisher** .... Check in position, secure and serviceable (gauge at top should be in green arc).

15. **Cockpit** .... Check for and remove/stow any loose articles.

16. **Upon leaving cockpit *do not* tread on flap surface.**

External

Begin at rear of wing. This should also be where you complete your checks.

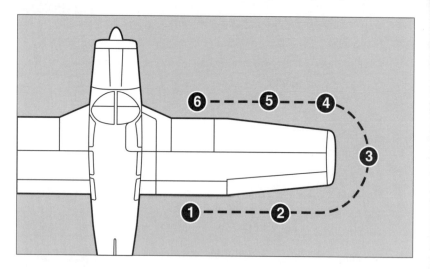

Starboard Wing

1. **Flap** .... Check upper and lower surface condition. Particularly check inner lower surface for caked mud or stone damage from wheels. Check linkage is secure and greased.

2. **Aileron** .... Check upper and lower surface condition, linkage and hinges secure. With fingers inside hinge line (hold the aileron with other hand), check balance weight is secure (inside wing tip). Check full and free movement—*do not use force.*

3. **Wing Tip** .... Check condition, security. Navigation light unbroken. (This area is particularly vulnerable to hanger damage.)

4. **Wing Surface** .... Check upper and lower surface condition.

5. **Wing Leading Edge** .... Check for dents along entire length.

6. **Fuel Tank** .... Check contents visually, resecure cap. Check fuel vent unblocked. Take fuel drain sample from under tank if necessary—check for correct color, water bubbles or sediment. Check that drain is not leaking.

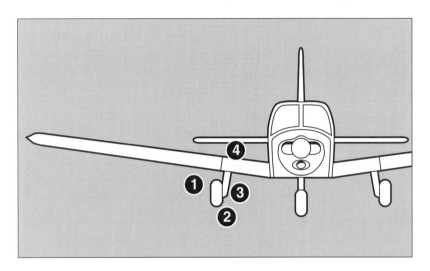

Starboard Landing Gear

1. **Tire** .... Check for tread and general condition. Check for correct inflation. Look for alignment of creep marks.

2. **Hydraulic Lines** .... Check for leaks (red fluid).

3. **Disc Brake** .... Should be shiny, not rusty or pitted.

4. **Oleo** .... Check extension. Look for mud or stone damage on wing and flap surface near landing gear.

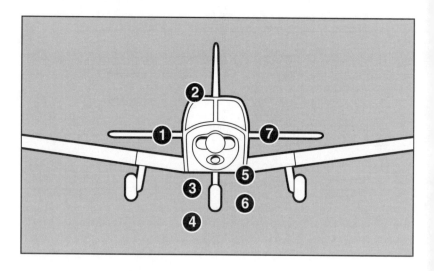

Front Fuselage and Engine

1. **Starboard Cowling** .... Open engine compartment, check oil level, *do not* overtighten dipstick on resecuring. Check engine compartment generally (i.e., HT leads secure, oil leaks). Resecure cowling.

2. **Windscreen** .... Should be clean and insect free, OAT probe secure.

3. **Nose Gear** .... Check oleo extension, linkage, nuts and split pins secure.

4. **Nose Wheel** .... Check for tread and general condition. Check for correct inflation. Check alignment of creep marks.

5. **Front Cowling** .... Check condition and security, intakes clear, landing light unbroken.

6. **Propeller** .... Look for cracks or chips, especially leading edge. Check spinner is secure and condition good. *Do not move or swing propeller.*

7. **Port Cowling** .... Open cowling and check brake fluid level. Check engine compartment (i.e., HT leads secure etc.). Resecure cowling. Take fuel sample. Check that fuel drain is not leaking.

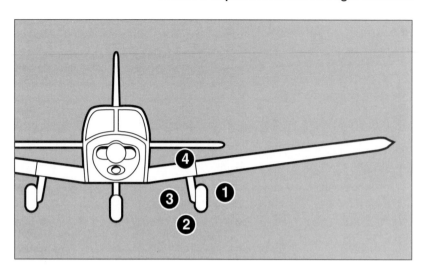

Port Landing Gear

1. **Tire** .... Check for tread and general condition. Check for correct inflation. Check alignment of creep marks.

2. **Hydraulic Lines** .... Check for leaks (red fluid).

3. **Disc Brake** .... Should be shiny, not rusty or pitted.

4. **Oleo** .... Check for correct extension. Look for mud or stone damage on wing and flap surface near landing gear.

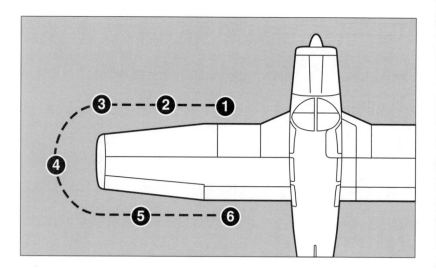

Port Wing

1. **Fuel Tank** .... Check contents visually, resecure cap. Take fuel drain sample if necessary. Check drain not leaking.

2. **Wing Leading Edge** .... Check for dents along entire length. Check pitot tube—*do not blow into perforations.*

3. **Wing Surface** .... Check upper and lower surface condition.

4. **Wing Tip** .... Check condition, security. Navigation light unbroken.

5. **Aileron** .... Check upper and lower surface condition, linkage and hinges secure, balance weight (inside wing tip) secure. Remember to watch for aileron movement while checking inside hinge line. Check full and free movement gently—*do not use force.*

6. **Flap** .... Check upper and lower surface condition especially near landing gear. Check linkage secure and greased.

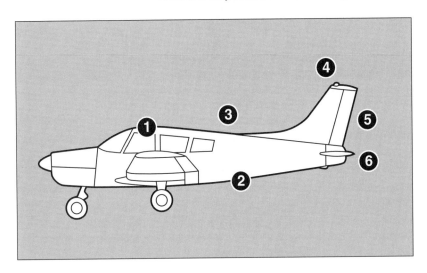

Port Fuselage

1. **Windows** .... Check clean and uncracked.

2. **Skin** .... Check general surface condition upper and lower, look for wrinkles, dents or punctures.

3. **Radio Antennas** .... Check secure.

4. **Tail Fin** .... Check skin condition, especially fairings; check antennas and rotating beacon secure.

5. **Rudder** .... Check condition, linkage secure and greased, nuts and split pins secure, nav light unbroken. *Do not attempt to force rudder movement.*

6. **Stabilator** .... Check upper and lower surface condition. Check linkage and split pins. Check full and free movement—*do not use force*. Ensure anti-balance tab moves in correct direction. Check other side of tail fin.

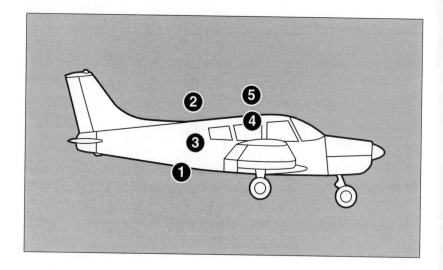

Starboard Fuselage

1. **Skin** .... Check general surface condition, upper and lower, look for any wrinkles, dents or punctures.

2. **Radio Antennas** .... Check secure. Do not tread on flap surface.

3. **Baggage Door** .... Check secure.

4. **Cockpit door** .... Check latches and hinges secure.

5. **Windows** .... Check clean and uncracked.

IMPORTANT

Remember: Full reference must be made to airplane flight manual, Pilot's Operating Handbook, flight school syllabus, etc., for all normal and emergency procedures.

If in doubt—ask

Section 6
Loading and Performance

Loading

Aircraft loading can be divided into two areas, the aircraft weight and the center of gravity (CG) position.

The aircraft must be loaded so that its weight is below the certified maximum takeoff weight (2,440 lbs for the Warrior II or 2,550 lbs for the Archer II). The flight manual may also list a "ramp weight," which is the maximum permissible weight for taxiing prior to takeoff. The difference between this and the maximum takeoff weight allows for the fuel used in taxiing and power checks. The weight limit is set primarily as a function of the lifting capability of the aircraft, which is largely determined by the wing design and engine power of the aircraft. Operating the aircraft when it is overweight will adversely effect the aircraft handling and performance, such as:

> Increased takeoff speed and slower acceleration
>
> Increased runway length required for takeoff
>
> Reduced rate of climb
>
> Reduced maximum altitude capability
>
> Reduced range and endurance
>
> Reduction in maneuverability and controllability
>
> Increased stall speed
>
> Increased approach and landing speed
>
> Increased runway length required for landing

The aircraft must also be loaded to ensure that its center of gravity (CG) is within set limits, normally defined as a forward and aft limit in inches aft of the datum. The forward limit is determined by the amount of elevator control available at landing speed; the aft limit is determined by the stability and controllability of the aircraft while maneuvering. Attempted flight with the CG position outside of the set limits (either forward or aft) will lead to control difficulties, and quite possibly loss of control of the aircraft.

When loading the aircraft it is standard practice to calculate the weight and CG position of the aircraft at the same time, commonly known as the weight and balance calculation. Before going further it must be emphasized that the following examples are provided for illustrative purposes only. Each individual aircraft has an individual weight and balance record that is valid only for that aircraft, and is dependent, among other things, on the equipment installed in the aircraft. If the aircraft has any major modification, repair or new equipment installed, a new weight and balance record will be produced. Therefore, in any loading or performance calculations, you must use the documents for the specific aircraft you will be using. As well as setting out limits, the aircraft documents will also give arms for each item of loading. The arm is a distance from the aircraft datum to the item. The weight multiplied by its arm gives its moment. Thus a set weight will have a greater moment the further away it is from the datum.

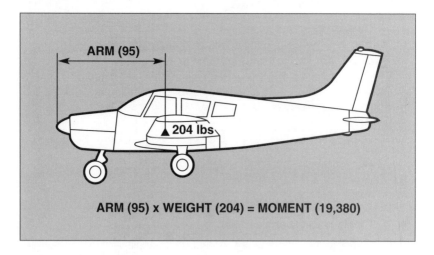

ARM (95) x WEIGHT (204) = MOMENT (19,380)

The operating weight of the aircraft can be split into two categories:

EMPTY WEIGHT—the weight of the aircraft, including unusable fuel; normally this includes full oil as well. The weight and CG position of the aircraft in this condition will be noted in the weight and balance record.

USEFUL LOAD—weight of the pilot, passengers, usable fuel and baggage. Again the weight and balance record will give an arm for each of these loads.

Weight and Center of Gravity Record

Produced by:

Grosvenor Aviation Services (Engineering) Limited

Aircraft Type:

Piper PA-38-112

Nationality and Registration Marks:

N-BGRR

Constructor's Serial Number:

78A0336

Maximum Permissible Weight:

1670 lbs

Maximum Landing Weight:

1670 lbs

Center of Gravity Limits:

Refer to Flight Manual Rep No. FAA 2126

All arms are distances in inches either fore or aft of datum.

Part "A" Basic Weight

The basic weight of this aircraft as calculated from Planeweighs Limited Report No. 1034 weighed on 08.07.88. at Manchester Airport is: **1182 lbs**

The center of gravity of aircraft in the same condition (aft of the datum) is: **74.66 inches**

The total Moment about the datum in this condition in lb inches is: **88254.45**

The DATUM referred to is defined in the Flight Manual, which is **66.25 inches** forward of wing leading edge.

The basic weight includes the weight of 12 lbs unusable fuel and 15 lbs of oil and the weight of items indicated in Appendix 1 which comprises the list of basic equipment carried.

Each individual aircraft has an individual weight and balance record, valid only for that aircraft.

Mathematical Weight and Balance Calculation

With this method of calculation the weights of each item are listed together with their arm. Addition of all the weights is the first step, to ensure that the resulting figure is within the maximum permitted. Assuming this is the case, the balance can then be calculated. For each item (except for the empty weight where the calculation is already done on the weight and balance record) the weight is multiplied by the arm, to give a moment. Normally the arm is aft of the datum, to give a positive figure. If the arm quoted is forward of the datum the moment will be negative (although obviously the weight is *not* deducted from the weight calculation). All the moments are then added together, to give the total moment, and this figure is then divided by the total weight. The resulting figure will be the position of the CG, which can be checked to ensure it is within the set limits. The weight and CG position can be plotted on a graph in the flight manual. If the plotted position is within the "envelope," the weight and CG position are within limits.

It is obviously important for the pilot to be sure of whether the aircraft needs to be operated in the NORMAL or UTILITY categories. The aircraft flight manual will advise which maneuvers can only be carried out when the aircraft is in the utility category. Operation in the utility category is defined as a reduced weight (2,070 lbs for the Warrior II, 2,130 lbs for the Archer II) and different CG limit. Also baggage in the rear baggage area and rear seat passengers are not permitted. The critical importance of the fuel load in the calculation of CG position for utility category operations should be remembered.

Example:

Empty Weight: Aircraft N-1234
From the weight and balance record for this aircraft, weight is 1514.90 lbs

Useful Load: Pilot 160 lbs
Co-Pilot 140 lbs
Fuel (level with tabs) 34 US gal @ 6.0 lbs
per US gal = 204 lbs

Although at this stage you can simply add together the weights to check the total weight, it is more common to make up a table to check weight *and* balance. Using the information above, and the arms from the weight and balance record, we can make up a table to calculate the moment for each item (remembering that weight x arm gives the moment).

ITEM	WEIGHT (lbs)	ARM (in)	MOMENT (lb-in)
Empty Weight: the weight, arm and moment are listed in the weight and balance record			
N-1234	1,514.9	87.13	131,993.00
Useful Load			
Pilot	160	80.5	12,880.00
Passenger	140	80.5	11,270.00
Fuel	204	95.0	19,380.00
Total Weight	2,018.9	Total Moment	175,523.00

The total weight is below the maximum permitted, and so is acceptable.

Dividing the total moment by the total weight gives the Center of Gravity position:

$$\frac{175,523.00}{2,018.9} = 86.94 \text{ inches aft of datum}$$

When this weight and CG position is plotted on the relevant graph in the flight manual, it can be seen that the aircraft is loaded to be within the UTILITY category.

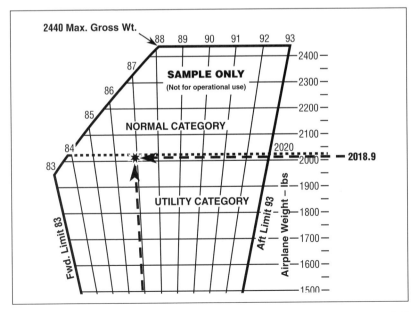

Out of interest, it is worth doing this exercise again, but now assuming full fuel, some rear passengers and a little baggage:

ITEM	WEIGHT (lbs)	ARM (in)	MOMENT (lb-in)
Empty Weight: the weight, arm and moment are listed in the weight and balance record			
N-1234	1514.9	87.13	131,993.00
Useful Load			
Pilot	160	80.5	12,880.00
Passenger	140	80.5	11,270.00
Fuel	288	95.0	27,360.00
2x Rear Seat Pax	300	118.1	35,430.00
Rear baggage	20	142.8	2,856.00
Total Weight 2,422.9		Total Moment 221,789.00	

The total weight is below the maximum permitted, although now we are out of the utility category and into the normal category.

Dividing the total moment by the total weight gives the Center of Gravity position:

$$\frac{221,789.00}{2,422.9} = 91.54 \text{ inches aft of datum}$$

When the weight and CG position is plotted on the graph in the flight manual, it can be seen that the aircraft is loaded to be within the NORMAL category. However, you can see that we are only allowing for some fairly light people and virtually no baggage. As Piper themselves point out, you are unlikely to be able to fill a Warrior with four adults, full fuel and full baggage and still be within limits. It is for the pilot-in-command to decide what to leave on the ground!

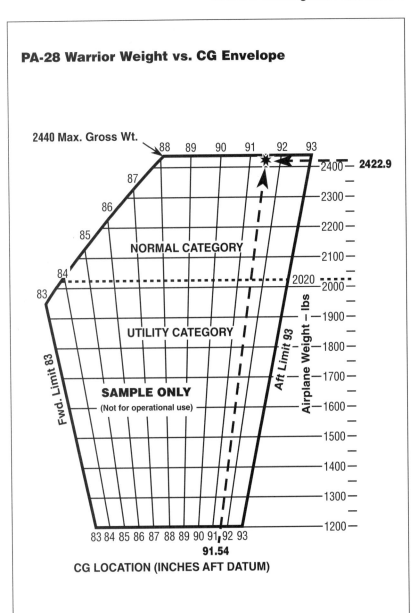

PA-28 Warrior Weight vs. CG Envelope

CG LOCATION (INCHES AFT DATUM)

Use of the Loading Graph

The problem with the mathematical methods is the time and amount of math involved. Here, the loading graph can help by multiplying the load by the arm for you. Using the figures from the second loading example before, the loading graph will look like this:

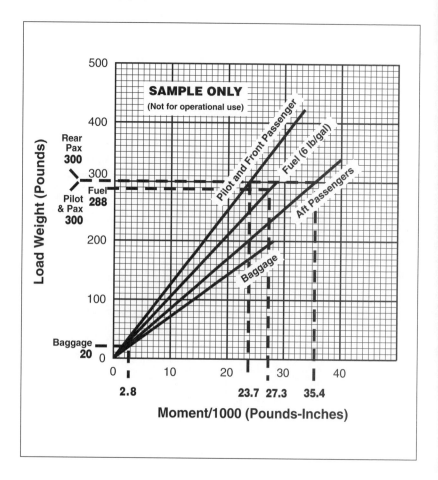

These figures can now go into a simplified table:

ITEM	WEIGHT	MOMENT/1000
N-1234	1,514.9	132
Pilot & Passenger	300	23.7
Fuel	288	27.3
Rear Passenger	300	35.4
Rear Baggage	20	2.8
Total Weight	2,422.9	Moment/1000 221.2

Again total moment (/1,000) is divided by total weight(/1,000)

$$\frac{221.2}{2.4229} = 91.29 \text{ inches aft of datum}$$

The slightly different result is due to the less exact nature of using the loading graph. If in any doubt, or if the result is close to the edge of the CG envelope, the mathematical method should be used.

A WORD OF WARNING. As well as the safety aspect, operating the aircraft outside its weight and balance envelope has far-reaching legal and financial implications. Almost the first thing an accident investigator will check after an accident is the loading of the aircraft. If the loading is outside limits, the pilot is violating the Federal Aviation Regulations. In addition, both the aircraft insurance company and your personal insurance company will be unsympathetic when they know that the conditions of the Airworthiness Certificate (i.e., the flight manual limitations) were not complied with. As the pilot-in-command, the responsibility is yours alone. The fact that the aircraft has four seats does not necessarily mean that the aircraft can be flown with all four seats occupied, baggage, and full fuel load.

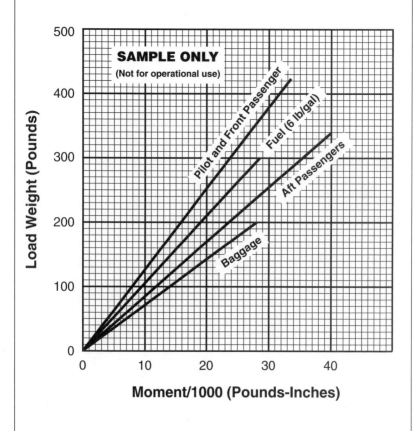

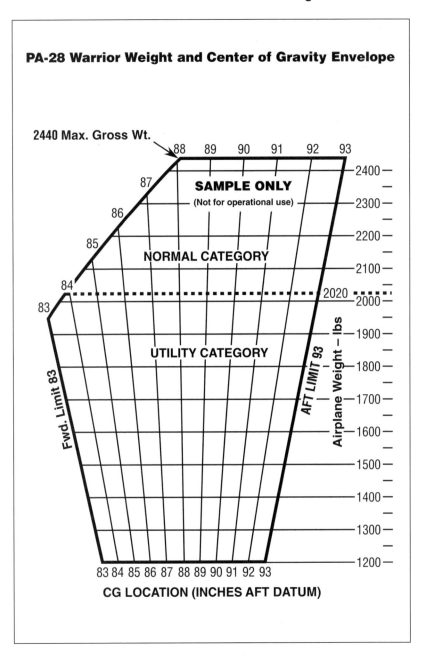

PA-28 Warrior Weight and Center of Gravity Envelope

2440 Max. Gross Wt.

SAMPLE ONLY
(Not for operational use)

NORMAL CATEGORY

2020

UTILITY CATEGORY

Fwd. Limit 83

AFT LIMIT 93

Airplane Weight – lbs

CG LOCATION (INCHES AFT DATUM)

Performance

The aircraft flight manual contains a section of graphs to allow the pilot to calculate the expected performance of the aircraft for different flight phases. The most commonly used graphs are those for takeoff and landing performance, and those are the ones we will concentrate on here. However, the same principles can be used on the other graphs. Two things to remember: First, the chart performance is obtained by using the recommended techniques—to get graph results follow chart procedures. Second, you can safely assume that the graph results have been obtained by placing a brand new aircraft in the hands of an experienced test pilot under favorable conditions. To make allowances for a less than new aircraft, being flown by an average mortal in the real conditions it is wise to "factor" any results you get. The charts may be "factored" to make allowances for the real world, and if so, the chart will be annotated as such. If not, some form of safety factoring is highly recommended. As with loading calculations, the pilot must use the graphs and data from the documents for the individual aircraft being used. The graphs and diagrams used in this section are for illustrative purposes only, and not for operational use.

In Section 7, conversion factors between feet and meters are listed, together with recommended factors for variations not necessarily covered by the flight manual graphs.

PA-28 Warrior Takeoff and Landing Performance Graphs

The takeoff distance and landing distance graphs in the flight manual make several assumptions (paved, level, dry runway; use of flight manual technique). Different graphs are provided for different flap settings for takeoff.

The graphs use the term "Pressure Altitude." This is the altitude of the runway assuming a standard pressure setting (i.e., 29.92" Hg). On a day with a pressure other than 29.92 you will need to adjust the actual altitude to get the pressure altitude. For instance on a day with a pressure above 29.92 the pressure altitude will be less than the actual, and vice versa. To do this conversion, simply adjust the actual altitude by 1,000 feet for each inch Hg above or below 29.92" (10 feet for each .01").

The headwind or tailwind component is calculated from the wind speed and the angle to the runway (i.e., a 10 knot wind directly down the runway gives a headwind component of 10 knots. A 10 knot wind at 90° to the runway gives a headwind component of 0). There is a graph in Section 7 for calculating head/tail wind component and crosswind component.

The takeoff distance and landing distance graphs will state the technique used to obtain the figures. Remember, to get graph results you have to use the graph techniques.

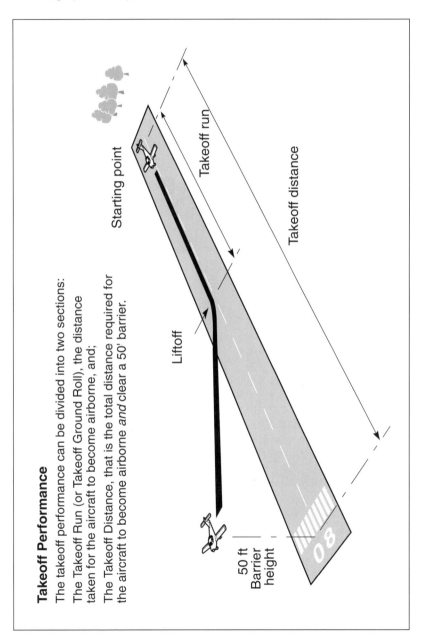

Takeoff Performance

The takeoff performance can be divided into two sections:

The Takeoff Run (or Takeoff Ground Roll), the distance taken for the aircraft to become airborne, and;

The Takeoff Distance, that is the total distance required for the aircraft to become airborne *and* clear a 50' barrier.

Takeoff Distance Calculation Example

For this example we will take the conditions as:

Outside Air Temperature +10°C
Pressure Altitude 1,200 feet
Takeoff weight 2,200 lbs
Headwind Component 5 Knots

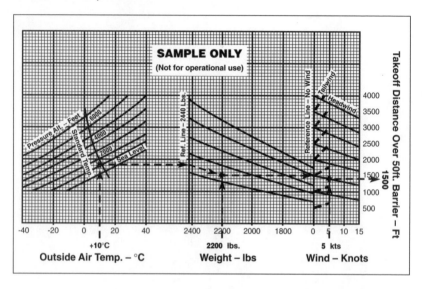

Start at the temperature +10°C, and then go vertically to the pressure altitude of 1,200 feet, then go horizontally to the REFERENCE LINE, and *then* parallel to the guideline until above the 2,200 lbs point. From this point take a line horizontally to the next reference line and then follow the guide line until above the 5 knots point. From this point take a line horizontally to the far side of the graph and read off the takeoff distance of 1,500 feet.

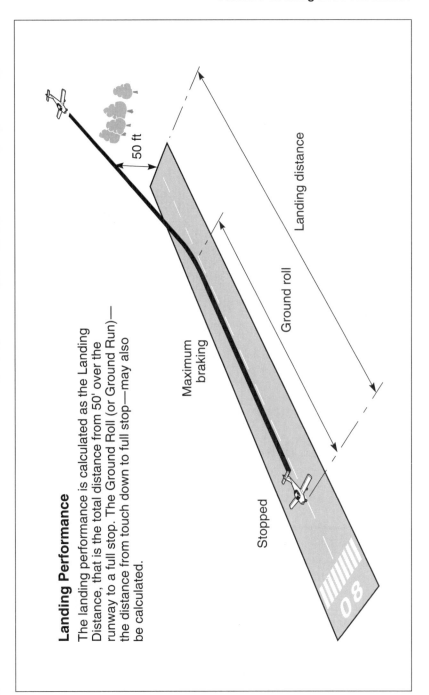

Landing Performance

The landing performance is calculated as the Landing Distance, that is the total distance from 50' over the runway to a full stop. The Ground Roll (or Ground Run)—the distance from touch down to full stop—may also be calculated.

50 ft

Landing distance

Ground roll

Maximum braking

Stopped

0 8

Landing Distance Calculation Example

For this example we will take the conditions as:

Outside Air Temperature +16°C
Pressure Altitude 1,000 feet
Landing weight 2,100 lbs
Headwind Component no wind

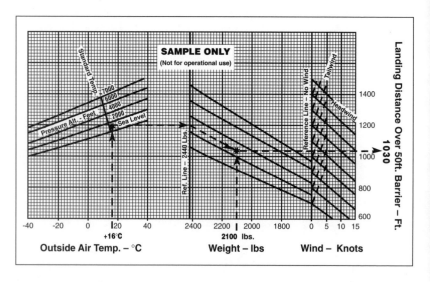

On the landing distance graph again start at the temperature (+16°C)
and go vertically to the pressure altitude (1,000 feet). From this point go
horizontally to the REFERENCE LINE, and then along the guideline until
above the 2,100 lbs point. Then go horizontally to the wind reference line.
As there is no wind carry on horizontally to the far side of the graph and
read off the landing distance in feet—1,030 feet.

En Route Performance

The aircraft flight manual contains graphs to enable en route performance, such as range and endurance, to be calculated. As already
covered, to get chart results, chart procedures must be used. In this case
the recommended leaning procedure is particularly relevant. Use of a
technique other than that in the flight manual will mean that chart results
are unlikely to be achieved.

PA-28 Warrior Takeoff Distance
Paved Level Dry runway, Flaps 25°

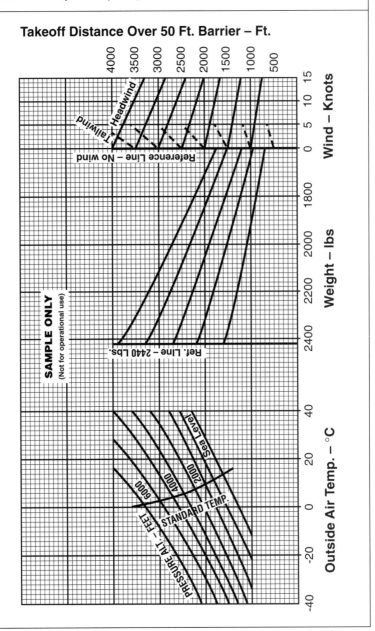

Takeoff Distance Over 50 Ft. Barrier – Ft.

SAMPLE ONLY
(Not for operational use)

PA-28 Warrior Landing Distance
Paved Level Dry Runway, Flaps 40°

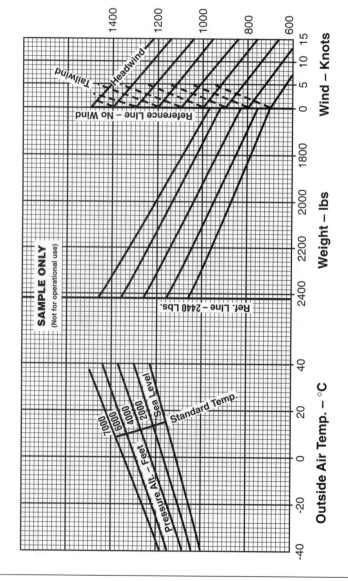

Landing Distance Over 50 Ft. Barrier – Ft.

Runway Dimensions

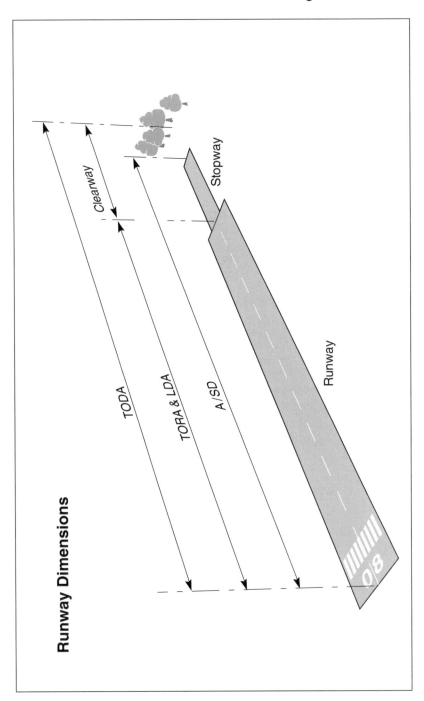

Runway Dimensions

Having calculated the distances the aircraft requires for takeoff or landing, the runway dimensions must be checked to ensure that the aircraft can be safely operated on the runway in question. The figures given in the Airport/Facility Directory or airfield guide can be defined in a number of ways.

The Takeoff Run Available (TORA)

The TORA is the length of the runway available for the takeoff ground run of the aircraft. This is usually the physical length of the runway.

The Accelerate/Stop Distance (A/SD)

The A/SD is the length of the TORA plus the length of any stopway. A stopway is an area at the end of the TORA prepared for an aircraft to stop on in the event of an abandoned takeoff.

The Takeoff Distance Available (TODA)

The TODA is the TORA plus the length of any clearway. A clearway is an area over which an aircraft may make its initial climb (to 50' in this instance).

The Landing Distance Available (LDA)

The LDA is the length of the runway available for the ground run of an aircraft landing. In all cases the landing distance required should never be greater than the landing distance available.

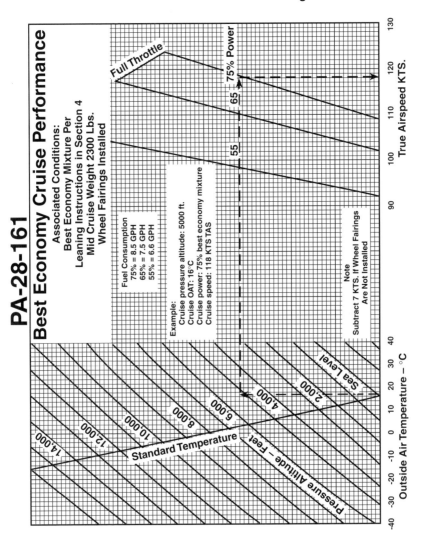

PA-28-161

Best Economy Cruise Performance

Associated Conditions:
Best Economy Mixture Per
Leaning Instructions in Section 4
Mid Cruise Weight 2300 Lbs.
Wheel Fairings Installed

Fuel Consumption
75% = 8.5 GPH
65% = 7.5 GPH
55% = 6.6 GPH

Example:
Cruise pressure altitude: 5000 ft.
Cruise OAT: 16°C
Cruise power: 75% best economy mixture
Cruise speed: 118 KTS TAS

Note
Subtract 7 KTS. If Wheel Fairings
Are Not Installed

Full Throttle

75% Power

75

65

55

Sea Level

2,000

4,000

6,000

8,000

10,000

12,000

14,000

Standard Temperature

Pressure Altitude – Feet

Outside Air Temperature – °C

True Airspeed KTS.

Section 7
Conversions

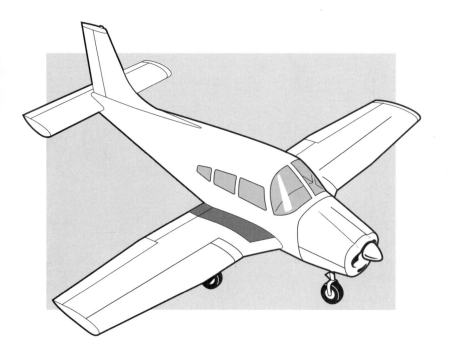

Takeoff Distance Factors

The following factors will allow the pilot to make allowance for variations
that may affect takeoff performance. Although some of these factors are
covered in the Warrior performance tables, the table is produced in its
entirety for completeness:

VARIATION	INCREASE IN TAKEOFF DISTANCE (to 50')	FACTOR
10% increase in aircraft weight	20%	1.2
Increase of 1,000' in runway altitude	10%	1.1
Increase in temperature of 10°C	10%	1.1
Dry Grass		
—Short (under 5 inches)	20%	1.2
—Long (5 – 10 inches)	25%	1.25
Wet Grass		
—Short	25%	1.25
—Long	30%	1.3
2% uphill slope	10%	1.1
Tailwind component of 10% of lift-off speed	20%	1.2
Soft ground or snow *	at least 25%	at least 1.25

* snow and other runway contamination are covered on page 7-5.

Landing Distance Factors

The following factors will allow the pilot to make allowance for variations that may affect landing performance. Although some of these factors are covered in the Warrior performance tables, the table is produced in its entirety for completeness:

VARIATION	INCREASE IN LANDING DISTANCE (from 50')	FACTOR
10% increase in aircraft weight	10%	1.1
Increase of 1,000' in runway altitude	5%	1.05
Increase in temperature of 10°C	5%	1.05
Dry Grass		
—Short (under 5 inches)	20%	1.2
—Long (5 – 10 inches)	30%	1.3
Wet Grass		
—Short	30%	1.3
—Long	40%	1.4
2% downhill slope	10%	1.1
Tailwind component of 10% of landing speed	20%	1.2
snow *	at least 25%	at least 1.25

* snow and other runway contamination are covered on page 7-5.

Runway Contamination

A runway can be contaminated by water, snow or slush. If operation on such a runway cannot be avoided additional allowance must be made for the problems such contamination may cause—i.e., additional drag, reduced braking performance (possible hydroplaning), and directional control problems.

It is generally recommended that takeoff should not be attempted if dry snow covers the runway to a depth of more than 2", or if water, slush or wet snow covers the runway to more than 1/2". In addition a tailwind, or crosswind component exceeding 10 knots, should not be accepted when operating on a slippery runway.

For takeoff distance required calculations, the other known conditions should be factored, and the accelerate/stop distance available on the runway should be at least 2.0 x the takeoff distance required (for a paved runway) or at least 2.66 x the takeoff distance required (for a grass runway).

Any water or slush can have a very adverse effect on landing performance, and the danger of hydroplaning (with negligible wheel braking and loss of directional control) is very real.

Use of the Wind Component Graph

This graph can be used to find the head/tail wind component and the crosswind component, given a particular wind velocity and runway direction.

EXAMPLE:

Runway 27

Surface wind 240°/15 knots

The angle between the runway direction (270°) and wind direction(240°) is 30°. Now on the graph locate a point on the 30° line, where it crosses the 15 knot arc. From this point take a horizontal line to give the headwind component (13 knots) and a vertical line to give the crosswind component (8 knots).

On the main graph overleaf the shaded area represents the maximum demonstrated crosswind component for this aircraft. If the wind point is within this shaded area, the maximum demonstrated cross-wind component for this aircraft has been exceeded.

Note:
Runway direction will be degrees magnetic. Check the wind direction given is also in degrees magnetic.

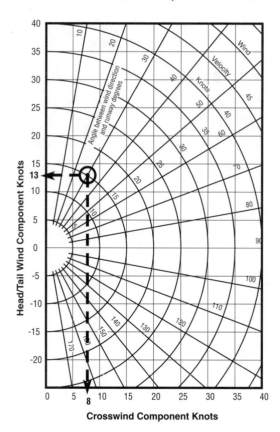

Crosswind Component Knots

Wind Component Graph

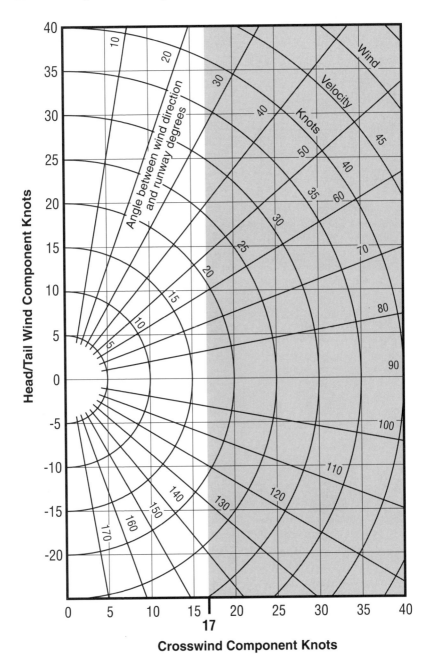

Crosswind Component Knots

Temperature

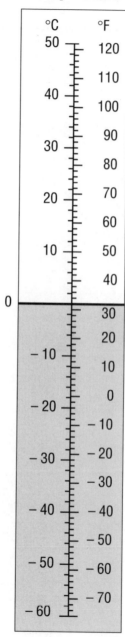

Distance – Meters/Feet

Meters	Feet		Feet	Meters
1	3.28		1	0.30
2	6.56		2	0.61
3	9.84		3	0.91
4	13.12		4	1.22
5	16.40		5	1.52
6	19.69		6	1.83
7	22.97		7	2.13
8	26.25		8	2.44
9	29.53		9	2.74
10	32.81		10	3.05
20	65.62		20	6.10
30	98.43		30	9.14
40	131.23		40	12.19
50	164.04		50	15.24
60	196.85		60	18.29
70	229.66		70	21.34
80	262.47		80	24.38
90	295.28		90	27.43
100	328.08		100	30.48
200	656.16		200	60.96
300	984.25		300	91.44
400	1,312.34		400	121.92
500	1,640.42		500	152.40
600	1,968.50		600	182.88
700	2,296.59		700	213.36
800	2,624.67		800	243.84
900	2,952.76		900	274.32
1,000	3,280.84		1,000	304.80
2,000	6,561.70		2,000	609.60
3,000	9,842.50		3,000	914.40
4,000	13,123.40		4,000	1,219.20
5,000	16,404.20		5,000	1,524.00
6,000	19,685.00		6,000	1,828.80
7,000	22,965.90		7,000	2,133.60
8,000	26,246.70		8,000	2,438.40
9,000	29,527.60		9,000	2,743.20
10,000	32,808.40		10,000	3,048.00

Conversion Factors:

Centimeters to Inches x .3937
Inches to Centimeters x 2.54

Meters to Feet x 3.28084
Feet to Meters x 0.3048

Distance – Nautical Miles / Statute Miles

NM	SM		SM	NM
1	1.15		1	.87
2	2.30		2	1.74
3	3.45		3	2.61
4	4.60		4	3.48
5	5.75		5	4.34
6	6.90		6	5.21
7	8.06		7	6.08
8	9.21		8	6.95
9	10.36		9	7.82
10	11.51		10	8.69
20	23.02		20	17.38
30	34.52		30	26.07
40	46.03		40	34.76
50	57.54		50	43.45
60	69.05		60	52.14
70	80.55		70	60.83
80	92.06		80	69.52
90	103.57		90	78.21
100	115.1		100	86.9
200	230.2		200	173.8
300	345.2		300	260.7
400	460.3		400	347.6
500	575.4		500	434.5
600	690.5		600	521.4
700	805.6		700	608.3
800	920.6		800	695.2
900	1035.7		900	782.1

Conversion Factors:

Statute Miles to Nautical Miles x 0.868976
Nautical Miles to Statute Miles x 1.15078

Volume (Fluid)

Liters	U.S. Gal.	U.S. Gal.	Liters
1	0.26	1	3.79
2	0.53	2	7.57
3	0.79	3	11.36
4	1.06	4	15.14
5	1.32	5	18.93
6	1.59	6	22.71
7	1.85	7	26.50
8	2.11	8	30.28
9	2.38	9	34.07
10	2.64	10	37.85
20	5.28	20	75.71
30	7.93	30	113.56
40	10.57	40	151.41
50	13.21	50	189.27
60	15.85	60	227.12
70	18.49	70	264.97
80	21.14	80	302.82
90	23.78	90	340.68
100	26.42	100	378.54
200	52.84		
300	79.26		
400	105.68		
500	132.10		
600	158.52		
700	184.94		
800	211.36		
900	237.78		
1000	264.20		

Conversion Factors:

U.S. Gallons to Liters x 3.78541
Liters to U.S. Gallons x 0.264179

PA-28 Warrior Index

Notes

Notes

Notes